Eric Hilton has been preaching on revival for many years and has experienced God working through his ministry time and time again.

It has been a great blessing for me to fellowship and pray with Eric at our Thursday evening prayer meetings. Eric always prays for revival which is desperately needed in our churches in USA, Canada and Europe. The great revivals of the past have come to America from Europe and have impacted the Founding Fathers of USA and Canada.

As you read this book on REVIVAL you will be impressed at the amount of research and documentation that Eric Hilton has given us on the subject of revival. He has also challenged our generation to begin to earnestly pray for revival and to ask God to begin it in us.

Dr. Bob Parschauer

If My People

Thoughts on Revival

EVANGELIST ERIC D. HILTON

WESTBOW
PRESS®
A DIVISION OF THOMAS NELSON
& ZONDERVAN

WestBow Press books may be ordered through booksellers or by contacting:

WestBow Press
A Division of Thomas Nelson & Zondervan
1663 Liberty Drive
Bloomington, IN 47403
www.westbowpress.com
1 (866) 928-1240

Cover Kelli Deconinck

Scripture quotations are from the King James Version of the Bible.

ISBN: 978-1-9736-9357-4 (sc)
ISBN: 978-1-9736-9358-1 (e)

Print information available on the last page.

WestBow Press rev. date: 7/10/2020

*D*edicated to my most gracious wife Cathy, a most precious gift from the loving hand of God.

Contents

Foreword ix

Preface xi

Chapter 1   The Meaning of Revival 1
Chapter 2   Prayer 16
Chapter 3   Preaching 28
Chapter 4   The word of God 38
Chapter 5   The Holy Spirit 47
Chapter 6   Worship 54
Chapter 7   Joy 58
Chapter 8   Unity 62
Chapter 9   Holiness 66
Chapter 10 Persecution 72
Chapter 11 Warfare 76
Chapter 12 Repentance 85
Chapter 13 Fear of the Lord 92
Chapter 14 Is Revival Needed? 98
Chapter 15 The Cross 104
Chapter 16 Hell 111
Chapter 17 The Church 116
Chapter 18 Evangelism 127
Chapter 19 Final Thoughts 136

Foreword

THROUGH THE MILES

We have been so privileged over the years and through the miles to have had the opportunity to bring the Good News of Jesus to the lost and at the same time bring encouragement to the saints.

Years ago when our children were young and we travelled long and far together we found ourselves in Kentucky primed for an old fashioned eight day tent revival. We not only sang and Eric preached but the children planned and presented the gospel through little skits to highlight the message. Wow,... we still reminisce how God moved in those meetings; many responded to the gospel and placed their faith in the Crucified One. One night an entire family came forward to declare their trust in the merits of Jesus. I recall how God gave our children the opportunity to counsel other young people about the decisions they made to follow Jesus.

My mind also goes back to a two week gospel crusade in the Philippines. We had the unique privilege as a family to preach and sing in many venues: outdoor services, in plazas, street markets, little bamboo churches, and the time we were invited to a large school. Just as we finished setting up, the electricity went out, (which was apparently not unusual) We then split up and we addressed individual classrooms. What a proud moment for Eric and I when we witnessed each of our children sharing the testimonies of their conversions and a life of serving Christ, and then they invited others to believe on Jesus for their salvation. Whole classrooms responded and our children prayed for them.

These are just a couple of precious moments from the past that linger in my mind but,... Christ is still the same, yesterday, today and forever. These memories are not meant to be like trophies on a shelf, but to remind us of the faithfulness of God. None of the wonderful stories of great movements of God are meant to simply be replayed as a broken record but to awaken a desire to see God lifted up and magnified once again. Because of this we are still travelling, still trusting, and still bringing forth the wonderful message that Jesus both saves and wants His church revived.

"But they that wait upon the Lord shall renew their strength; they shall mount up with wings as eagles; they shall run, and not be weary; and they shall walk, and not faint. " (Isaiah 40:31)

Cathy Lynn Hilton

Preface

hy write a book on revival? I will give you two reasons. The first reason is that the church in Canada and the USA is in a deplorable state! I see a horrible condition of sin sickness and soul disease. We need a remedy and God has it, revival. God admonished the church on four of the most difficult things to get Christians to do. If my people, which are called by my name, shall, 1. "humble themselves", 2. "pray", 3. "seek My face", and, 4. "turn from their wicked ways". You will, no doubt, notice the things that He does not mention... not giving, not praise and worship, not forming more committees, not more movie nights, not more concerts, not yard sales, not even more evangelism. We must not put the cart before the horse. We need God's healing, we need revival. Hear the promise, three results, 1. "then will I hear from heaven" 2. "and will forgive their sin" 3. "AND WILL HEAL THEIR LAND." (II Chronicles 7:14) This a promise from God and it's a good promise. I do not see any alternative other than this approach. Hence the title of this book, "If My People".

The second reason is, I have been spoiled by an incredible movement of God. It is one thing to write out of study, it is another to write out of experience.

Back in 1995 my wife Cathy and I were asked to come to a Christian youth camp to sing and preach. We arrived and it was evident some of the young people did not want to be there, and their aim was simply to disrupt the meeting. We proceeded as planned, we sang a few choruses and Cathy sang a few specials then I presented the gospel in the simplest way I knew how. It was not a particularly profound message, and it was not even dynamic but the Holy Spirit was secretly doing a work in each of the hearts of those present that evening. At the end of the message I asked, "Who wants to come to the cross and receive Jesus' forgiveness through His shed blood?". There were twenty five people there that night and twenty indicated they wanted to trust Christ. I did not think they fully understood, so I explained clearer and asked, "All those who wanted to rest their hope on the atonement through Jesus to stand to their feet!" This time twenty three young people stood to their feet as did their leaders. The disrupters were the first to jump to their feet. At this point I prayed for them and without any leading, suggestion or instruction from myself or Cathy, they all began weeping and sobbing. I never saw anything like this before, but I recognized the Holy Spirit was doing something. Did the Holy Spirit fall on these young people? Is this REVIVAL? So I said to Cathy, "Let's stand back, out of the way and let the Holy Spirit do His perfect work." The young people continued wailing with gut wrenching cries and then they began confessing sins one to another and one young lady told me she needed to confess to me. I told her she need not confess to me but she said she had to or she would burst. This went on for a half an hour or so. Some threw out CDs they deemed vile and young men tore up inappropriate T-shirts. We were told later that some sobbed most of the night.

This was the sovereign work of the Holy Spirit and we were privileged to witness it frequently that summer. I began preaching revivals and evangelism from that summer on but I have never experienced anything like it since. I have seen those that have experienced personal revival, I have seen some with brokenness and contrition but I have not quite seen a corporate move of God in the same way. I am hoping to, and I am praying God would let me see it again.

You might be asking, where are they now? I really do not know, they all went back to their home churches, most to "The Church of the Wet Blanket" and the church did the best they could to douse the flames of revival. But every now and then we will be recognized by someone who tells us they remember those meetings at the camp.

So this is a book that puts real revival into proper perspective. I do this by including poignant quotes from the great revivalists of the past, men like: Wesley, Whitefield, Edwards, Brainerd, Spurgeon, Ravenhill, Finney and others. I relate little stories of some of the great revivals of the past: The Great Awakening, The Welsh Revivals, The Hebrides Revival and others. I include personal stories and anecdotes from our own lives and experiences. I have also made sure to use the Bible as the firm foundation of all truths to be learned about revival. Anything else is empty and foolish.

My sincerest hope is that this little book will spark revival in your heart. If nothing else, I would be happy if it just got you thinking about revival, talking about revival and praying for revival. God bless you my dearest reader.

Eric D. Hilton.

Special thanks to my wonderful and really smart editor Linda Munroe. Everything correct and easy to read is because it has passed through her eyes and has been corrected or has met with her approval. Everything that is awkward or obscure is where she lost the argument and relented to allow me to write it as I wanted.

Eric D. Hilton

CHAPTER 1

The Meaning of Revival

he essence of true revival is when the outpouring of the Holy Spirit fills the recesses of the soul and there is an unmistaken realization of our own depravity and a deep abhorrence of self. Then grace appears with nail pierced hands and feet and with it a powerful motivation for repentance and an overwhelming desire for inward holiness.

- EDH

While this little book is not a "how to" book we must establish some definitions. What do we mean when we say the word revival?

There have been a great many definitions over the years so I will just mention a few. D.M. Panton wrote, "Revival—the inrush of the Spirit into a body that threatens to become a corpse."

Andrew Murray describes it like this. "The word revival means making alive again those who have been alive but have fallen into what is called a cold or dead state. They are Christians and have life, but they need reviving to bring them back to their first love and healthy growth of the spiritual life to which conversion was meant to be the entrance."

Edwin Orr the great revivalist of the mid twentieth century said, "An evangelical revival is an extraordinary work of God in which Christians repent of their sins as they become intensely aware of His presence in their midst and they manifest a positive response to God in renewed obedience to the known will of God, resulting in both a deepening of their individual and corporate experience with God, and an increased concern to win others to Christ."

In the year 1888 the Australian Christian World editorial wrote this, "No church that values its own standards can afford to depreciate revivals of religion. The whole world history of the Christian church from its foundation until now is a history of revivals. It should always be borne in mind that real revival is something more than a mere gale of religious excitement sweeping over the churches. A genuine revival is a manifestation of the supernatural and divine power."

It can be accurately said, revival is the moving of the Holy Spirit in our hearts, where by we begin to place our deepest and fondest love in the precious Lord Jesus. But some will say, "O how I love the Christ of Calvary!" Then Jesus pierces us through with the penetrating question, "Lovest thou me more than these?" (John 21:15) What are our "these"? We must all come to the place where we examine who or what has real possession of our heart. We can only dance with one partner and the one we dance with the most is the one we love the most.

Without contradiction, to put it very simply, revival is having God in His rightful place. That is, that God would be preeminent in our lives, our church and in our community. You see, my dear reader, revival is all about transformation. Revival transforms lightweight believers into solid Christians. A feather is light, and it is fluffy, and wherever it lands it makes no impact. Most of our Christianity can be described in that way. Ask yourself, "Am I making an impact in my workplace, my school, my community, in my business, etc?" Oh, you have studied much, you know your theology but has the world seen a demonstration of authentic Christianity in you? Someone has asked this question and I think it bears repeating. If you were arrested for being a Christian would there be enough evidence to convict you? Revival heat tempers us into the bold imprint of Jesus. The Jewish leaders took one look at Peter and John and listened to them and they reported saying, "... they took knowledge of them, that they had been with Jesus." (Acts 4:13) A soul revived is living salt and light.

K. Malcomson put it like this, "Revival is radical! You cannot be touched by revival and be the same. Revival radically changes lives. It is more than experience, manifestations, visions or feelings. It is Christ revealed to us, in us and through us."

Inception

Revival begins with God's own people; the Holy Spirit touches their heart anew, and gives them new fervour and compassion, zeal, new light and life. And when He has thus come to you, He next goes forth to the valley of dry bones... Oh, what responsibility this lays on the church of God! If you grieve Him away from yourself, or hinder His visit, then the poor perishing world suffers sorely.

- Andrew Bonar

Revival when conceived must then be nurtured in embryo with much prayer. But it is imperative we begin by forsaking all corruptness of heart and mind repenting of all known sins and questionable habits. May we then devote ourselves to feeding on the sincere milk of the word and by drinking in the breath of the Holy Spirit. Set apart time to intelligently, intentionally and intensely to pray for just revival. When Zion travailed she bringeth forth children. (Is 66:8)

It is my observation that in times of revival the Holy Spirit makes sin very personal. It is never enough to know about the exceeding sinfulness of sin, the offence of sin must be felt. I could know fire is hot but I cannot fully know its effect until I have felt its heat. David cried, "Against thee, thee only, have I sinned, and done this evil in thy sight,..." (Psalms 51:4). Like a skilled physician the Holy Spirit breaks the bone so He can set it right. "That the bones which thou hast broken may rejoice." (Psalms 51:8)

I will also tell you what revival is not (there are numerous misconceptions), revival is not a smokin' hot praise and worship band that gives you warm and fuzzy feelings and goose bumps. Some of our worship teams bring just the opposite effect of ushering in revival. We sometimes mistake talent for anointing, volume for presence and brilliance for blessing and this is precarious. Some worship teams are amazing but very worldly and some of the women dress immodestly. In some cases I believe we could be guilty of idolatry; worshiping our worship and falling prostrate before our presentations. And while I am not saying this is true for every church I am saying we must be careful we do not mistake "the trends" as being revival. Look at some of our major Christian recording artists, across the genres. Why, I wouldn't give you five cents for the walk of some of them today. Make no mistake about it while what I have just described may draw the biggest crowds, God is not pleased nor will He ever be pleased.

The cry of every blood bought, born again, soldier of the living God is not, "more money, flashier ministries, greater music, better Christian movies or even more missionaries!" It must be! It has to be, "REVIVE US AGAIN", and yet, how many have given up five minutes to spend at the throne of grace to beg almighty God for this all important need.

Revival is not all about manifestations. Now, when the Holy Spirit is poured out there is an overwhelming sense of His presence. He is an all reaching, all powerful, all searching God and coming in contact with Him does create a reaction like hot oil submerged in cold water. When someone sticks their finger in a light socket there is a reaction. But we can mistake reaction for revival. True revival always brings about true repentance; a bitterness of soul. God is not impressed with the amount of tears we shed or the deep contrition we feel if it is not accompanied by the renouncing of sin and turning to, or returning to God wholeheartedly, full hog, without reserve, right down to the last bristle of the tail. Revival and repentance are Siamese twins, indivisible, they are joined at the mind, the heart and the soul. To remove repentance is to kill revival.

Why do we continue to try to arouse the church without God? We can sink all kinds of money and energy into all kinds of programs and church improvements but what we need is revival. 1Corinthians 3:10 describe the efforts of man, "Wood, hay and stubble!" This is what man plants, nurtures and harvests. Then man can pat himself on the back, and say, "Look what I have done!"...but the Bible says, these works will be tested by fire. (v15) Every work which is only designed to be seen of men will perish. Gold, silver, precious stones, this bounty God places in the womb of the earth and man has only to search for it. Revival is available to His church, and is essential to His Church, if we would only repent and seek it. It will also be tested with fire but revival fire will purify these elements. Revival God's way with God's provisions will always stand the test.

The evangelist/preacher does not, cannot, will not bring revival. He preaches revival, but he does not bring it. This, is of course, no excuse for laziness in study, nor licence for weak lily-livered, milk toast preaching, but even if he could preach with the tongue of Spurgeon and the passion of Whitefield, revival would not be automatic. It is still the Holy Spirit who reproves of sin, righteousness and judgement. (John 16:8) The greatest effort in revival is when he, the preacher, and the church is on its knees in humble prayer.

Revival must never be a sanctified pep rally led by sanctified cheer leaders. This detestable practise pumps up the flesh like a hyper-enthusiastic sales meeting, but deflates as quickly as the preacher breathes his last Amen. It is the Spirit that quickeneth [revives]. The flesh profiteth nothing. (John 6:63) This type of revival may boast of much but delivers little. It delights the senses but the spirit remains dormant. Oh, how we need sweet manna from heaven, only this will invigorate a hungry soul.

Authentic revival typically is not a carbon copy of other moves of God but, there are always some components that are common. Never, ever, let us forget that revival is always based on the reality of the redemption. O how we need a fresh vision of the cross, without it we have nothing but husks; it will not revive, it will not waken a sleeping soul. "Next", as Andrew Bonar wrote, "God's program for reviving His people is definite and clear. First Elijah repaired the altar of Jehovah that was thrown down. That is the place to begin. All the ruin that sin has made wrought must be cleared by confession. Things must be made right with God: restitution must be made where due. Unless this is done definitely and thoroughly, prayer for reviving is vain. Too many are praying without repairing the altar by confession of sin, without digging a trench of separation from the world and without a surrender that is even death. No wonder such prayer is fruitless."

But someone will say, "Revival, what of it? The evangelist comes, delivers a thunderous sermon, people come forward and where are they two months later? They are back in the bars, they are back with their bad crowds; their decisions were mere emotion; they did not last." And I reply, "That is not revival! Where there is true revival, there is no such thing as backsliding. He who was formerly the drunk is now in the prayer meeting, and she who was formerly the adulteress now sings on the praise team. Oh, there may be some whose profession is not real, but why throw the baby out with the bath water?" I am aware there are evangelists who can preach bold and eloquent, but they can also neglect Jesus (much thunder, no rain). They can have the altar full, but if it be the cords of man that draws men, man will quickly break it. Jesus said, "And I, if I be lifted up from the earth, will draw all men unto me." (John 12:32) Therein lies the difference.

Does Jesus Christ deserve our lacklustre praise, halfhearted worship, lukewarm service, drowsy attentiveness and our blatant disobedience? We often think revival is supposed to be for us: to get us excited, to improve our Christian experience, to help our church and our community... No, no,... revival is all for Him. "Jesus paid it all, all to Him I owe!" I do not want revival for revival sake, I want revival so Jesus will be exalted higher, Jesus will magnified bigger, Jesus will be glorified brighter! There can be no revival until we get hold of this one truth,... He is worthy!

I have heard the dolorous cries, "I have strayed from the path!"... Jesus is the way: that is revival. "I have swallowed lies!"... Jesus is the truth: that is revival. "I am dead!"... Jesus is the life: that is revival. "I have taken a thousand steps out of the way." Yes, but it is only one step to come back. "I have embraced a thousand lies." Yes, but it is one truth to come back. "I feel as dead as a graveyard, as dull and lifeless as a tombstone." Yes, but there still is life in the crucified one. Revival is in a person!... the Lord Jesus Christ. ".... I am the way, the truth and the life..." (John 14:6)

A couple of pastors considering our ministry expressed concern, indicating, they weren't to sure about our focus on revival. Would revival be injurious to the flock? Is the promotion of revival noxious to the church? Some people believe that revival is more like a cause. I tell you, it is not! They seem to think there is a shift, from the worship of God to the worship of revival. I assure you, nothing could be farther from the truth. They think there is an exclusion of Jesus and we become mere enthusiasts of the Spirit. This too is false, however, these errors have happened. There are those who would embrace an experience rather than the Saviour. True revival fulfills the greatest need for man today, to have a revelation of the reality of the redemption.

Revival sometimes comes in drips and spits, like the little scattered sprinklings on parched ground. I have often seen how the Holy Spirit has worked sovereignly in individual hearts and has brought about personal revival. Other times revival comes as a divine shower. Abundance of rain on a dry and thirsty land. The Holy Spirit being poured out on the entire meeting place. I have also had the pleasure of witnessing this type of outpouring of God, resulting in corporate revival. Then, there are times when there is a deluge, like the mighty flood waters that break their dykes into pieces and march uninhibited through the streets. This is an intense, powerful move of God, when the heavens are no longer as brass and God does rend the heavens and comes down. In times like these, revival is poured out on an entire community. Church history is replete with many instances of such wonderful manifestations of God. I have not yet seen it but I long to; I expect to.

J.C. Smith observes the blessedness of revival, he, being present during the times when M'Cheyne and Burns preached. "In these moments or times of revival, when the blessed Holy Spirit draws near to the people of God in power and in love, our hearts are lifted above the world, our souls pant after God, the living God, and much of our time is spent in adoring and admiring the bleeding lamb, who died on Calvary. The believer in these times of revival begins again. He gets up a step, and goes from faith to faith, from strength to strength, from profession to reality, from twilight gloom to the morning of peace and joy."

"O! men and brethren, what would this heart feel if I could believe that there were some among you who would go home and pray for revival, men whose faith is large enough, and their love fiery enough to lead them from this moment to exercise unceasing intercessions that God would appear among us and do wondrous things here, as in times of former generations." -CH Spurgeon

Awakening

"When sinners are careless and stupid, and sinking into hell unconcerned. It is time the church should bestir themselves. It is as much the duty of the church to awake, as it is for the fireman to awake when a fire breaks out in the night of a great city."

-Charles Finney

The preachers of old spoke often of the stage of awakening, (we don't talk about it anymore). Awakening, is the realization of being lost, one sees they are in a desperate condition; there is a sense that they are doomed; they are convinced they are hell deserving sinners. The law has smitten them, the Holy Spirit has convicted and the word has pierced them through. Awakening is not salvation but it precedes it. Someone could move from being awakened to salvation in minutes or it could take years or never. Most people during highly emotional evangelistic services are awakened. They raise their hand during an invitation, they say a prayer at an altar, sign a card, but many have only felt the conviction of sin, or some just respond out of curiosity or out of enthusiasm. The awakened sinner tries many means to feel relief: reforms, keeping of the law, tears, remorse, church attendance, good deeds etc. but all to no avail. The awakened sinner immediately converts to the Christian belief system: Bible reading, church attendance, and the like. There are none that naturally seek after God but when there is an awakening they hear the voice of God saying, "Seek ye the Lord while He may be found, call ye upon Him while He is near" (Isaiah 55:6) and in the awakened state they are driven to the cross. The Holy Spirit opens the mind to the veracity of scripture and wins the heart to true faith in Jesus.

God's prescription for salvation is the blood of Jesus. Salvation, is only apprehended by faith when the sinner comes with all their sin to the place of the cross, "... before whose eyes Jesus Christ hath been evidently set forth and crucified..." for them! Personal.(Galatians 3:10) Awakening brings tears of sorrow but salvation brings tears of joy. I believe there are multitudes in Christian churches who profess to be born again but there is no possession.

Awakening is what we bring to salvation: our tears, deep contrition, repentance, devotion, good deeds, surrender, and so forth. Salvation is what we get from God, "Then will I sprinkle clean water upon you, and ye shall be clean; from all your filthiest, and from all your idols, I will cleanse you. A new heart also will I give you and a new spirit will I put within you: and I will take away the stony heart out of your flesh, and I will give you an heart of flesh." (Ezekiel 36:25, 26) Awakening must precede salvation, it is absolutely necessary, but it does not bring it. True salvation is all of grace. The sinner must come to the only ground on which sinful man and a holy God can meet, and that is at Calvary's cross, where the Lamb of God was slain for our sin. For [God] made [Jesus] to be sin for us,who knew no sin; that we might be made the righteousness of God in Him (2Corinthians 5:21). I believe this is where much fog exists. Multitudes come forward at an evangelistic crusade, the message is heard, the message is believed, it begins to make sense, they come with sincerity and tears. They ask, "What must I do?" Even though the message is "Look and live" all they understand at this point is, "come forward, repeat a prayer or sign a card". So they do. Is that salvation? No! This is an essential stage but, many are only awakened or in the first stages of conversion.

David said in Psalm 51, "Restore unto me the joy of thy salvation and uphold me with Thy free spirit. Then will I teach transgressors Thy way and sinners shall be converted." (Psalms 51:8) David understood, a restored, revived, backslidden sinner like him, was the way to see others awakened and saved

The parable of the sower also gives us additional insight. Look at the seed sown on the stony places, "And some fell upon a rock; and as soon as it was sprung up, it withered away, because it lacked moisture." (Luke 8:6). Matthew says, "where they had not much earth, and forthwith they sprung up, because they had no deepness of earth, and when the sun was up, they withered away." (Matthew 13:5,6) That is, as Jesus explains, "Those on the rock are they, which, when they hear, receive the word with joy; and these have no root, which for a while believe, and in time of temptation fall away." (Luke 8:13) Notice, they hear the word, they receive the word, they respond to the word, they are "awakened" but they have not moved on to the new birth and do not last.

So, awakening, and conversion are essential to salvation, like repentance is essential to salvation, but all the repenting in the world will not bring salvation. Salvation is through the precious blood of Jesus Christ. "But as many as received Him, to them gave He power to become the sons of God, even to those who believe on His name." (John 1:12). We are brought into the family of God by grace alone (solo gratia) through "FAITH" alone (solo fida) on the merits of Jesus Christ alone (solo Christus) to the glory of God (Deo gloria).

We see the law fulfilled in Christ, wrath appeased, death destroyed, sin forgiven, my soul saved.

In the gospel of John we learn the doctrine of the new birth from Jesus, when he taught Nicodemus, Jesus said, "Except a man be born again, he cannot see the kingdom of God. Nicodemus saith unto him, how can a man be born when he is old? Can he enter the second time into his mother's womb and be born?" (Jn. 3:4,5) A question based on the flesh, for even if that were possible it would still be the same mother and the same sin nature inherited from our first parents. "That which is born of the flesh is flesh: and that which is born of the spirit is spirit." (v. 5) We must be born of the Spirit and receive a new nature, the divine nature from righteous Jesus.

I believe there are multitudes, sitting in church pews or chairs who have been awakened, that is, they adhere to the belief system of Christianity. They might have been converted from, Islam, Hinduism, Satanism, atheism or whatever, but are not saved. This answers the question of falling away. Many would say the church members have lost their salvation. Which, to my view, is impossible. Whosoever believeth on Him hath everlasting life. If someone could lose their salvation it would not be everlasting. It is however, conceivable that there may be many awakenings, but there can only be one new birth.

"Evermore", writes Charles Finney, "the law must prepare the way for the gospel. Failure to use the law in converting souls is almost certain to lead to a false standard of Christian experience and to fill the church with false converts." Mr Finney wrote this over two hundred years ago and I believe we are now at the stage in Christian history he spoke of.

There are two lies that enter the mind of an awakened sinner:

1. "God could never forgive someone like you, you are so filthy, wicked and unworthy." This is a demonic half truth. We are all filthy, wicked and unworthy. We have all sinned and have fallen short of the glory of God. We have all been anarchists in our heart and have declared, "We will not have this man

to reign over us." The lie is, God could never forgive us. Oh! Praise His holy name. "For the Son of Man is come to seek and save that which was lost." (Luke 19:10) "I came not to call the righteous but sinners to repentance." (Luke 5:32) "For when we were yet without strength, in due time Christ died for the ungodly." (Romans 5:6) Dear friend, the devil could tell you a lot of things but he cannot tell you you are not ungodly, sinful, weak or lost.

2. The second lie is aimed at the false convert designed to convince them they are saved. They perceive their standing is on good ground but it is sinking sand. They are affirmed by others, "My,... look at how wonderful you are. God loves you so much, you are on your way to heaven. Keep up the good work, the formality etc." in this way the foul fiend flatters. To him, you can be a church attendee, you can be conservative, you can be pro life, just not born again. The first lie the awakened sinner overcomes at the cross when he hears the word, "Come now let us reason together, saith the Lord. Though your sins be as scarlet, they shall be as white as snow; though they be red like crimson, they shall be as white as wool." (Isaiah 1:18) "In whom" the Bible says, "we have redemption through his blood, the forgiveness of sin..." (Ephesians 1:7) We are invited to come to the cross with just our sin, saying "Nothing in my hand I bring, simply to the cross I cling." Simple child like faith. The second lie is perilous. They must be convinced of their doleful estate. "For I have not known sin but by the law." (Romans. 7:7) The law was our schoolmaster to bring us unto Christ, that we might be justified by faith. (Galatians 3:24) Revival kicks out all the scaffolding to reveal which way we lean, if it is not on the all sufficiency of Christ through the redemptive work, we are on rotting boards suspended over hell and they will not hold. What are we trusting in?

There is yet another type of awakening, and this for the child of God. There are multitudes in Christian churches who are asleep spiritually. Think of what can happen while someone sleeps. A knife could be held to the throat of a sleeper, but they are completely defenceless. Their house could be on fire, but they are completely unaware. They could be robbed by a thief but they are totally oblivious. And, there is nothing worse than the driver who nods off while behind the wheel, it means destruction. Samson, the great champion of Israel, lost his locks while he slept on the lap of carnal security. (Spurgeon) "... and wist not that the Lord was departed from him.(Judges 16:20) Look at how many are defenceless to the enemies's onslaught, they are ignorant of Satan's devices, and they are impervious to any sensibility of the the work and wonder of God. Look!... One Armed Arnold has learned to live without an arm!... Glass eyed Glenda has learned to live without an eye!... but have learned to live without the power of God... asleep at the wheel? Without the power of God we are no different from the world: in our actions, our responses, our reactions in crisis. God forbid that we should feel normal and be without the power of God. Only personal revival will shake us out of such a deplorable state. Isaiah shouts to the congregation in his day, "AWAKE, AWAKE put on strength". (Is. 52:1)

There are many Christians who have travelled far and long on the pathway of God. Weary they enter the segment of the journey which John Bunyan describes as the enchanted ground. It is a place where lack of watchfulness and false contentment leads to lethargy, apathy, indolence, and indifference. It is here where the pilgrims (in Pilgrim's Progress) comes across Heedless and Too-Bold, who sadly sat down to rest themselves and so fell asleep. Hear the word of REVIVAL all who are making "The Enchanted Ground" their present dwelling. AWAKE, AWAKE! "Let us not sleep as others, but let us watch and be sober". (1Thessalonians 5:6)

This is precisely what took place on July 8th 1741 in the Enfield Connecticut congregation. The preacher, Jonathan Edwards preached

13

a powerful sermon, "Sinners in the Hands of an Angry God." Before the sermon was finished, people were moaning, groaning, and crying out such things as, "What shall I do to be saved?" It was reported by another minister who witnessed the service that, "there was such a breathing of distress and weeping, that the preacher was obliged to speak to the people and desired silence that he might be heard." These were churched people but the Holy Spirit descended upon the church and the "Great Awakening" was sparked.

There have been instances in the history of the church when the telling and retelling of the wonderful works of God have been used to rekindle the expectation of faithful intercession and prepare the way for another Awakening.

- J. Edwin Orr

PENTECOSTAL POWER

Lord, as of old at Pentecost
thou didst thy power display,
With cleansing, purifying flame descend on us today,
Lord, send the old time power, the Pentecostal power!
Thy flood gates of blessing on us throw open wide!
Lord, send the old time power, the Pentecostal power,
That sinners be converted and Thy name glorified!

- Charlotte G. Homer. (1856)

HOLY HUM

Old saint of sixty years; voice trembles as he prays.
He uses "thee's" and "thou's"
before the throne of grace;
Relives the days of long ago, when revival fire came.
And he begs the Lord his God he'd do it once again.

Holy hum, Lord, thy kingdom come.
Holy hum, Lord, thy will be done.
My heart's anticipating;
The church is resonating.
With a holy hum.

The young man in the front row a week ago got saved,
He talks to the Lord, "How you doing today?
I really have to ask you Lord, I hope I don't offend.
But I am so burdened for my dear lost friends."

The woman in the back row, with a tissue to her eye, She
whispers out a desperate plea beneath a humble cry
"My child's so weak they all say, "his life is almost gone,'
But I know that you are able, so I lift him to the throne."

We all have different stories but we're in one accord.
With one heart and one mind like incense heavenward.
Holy Hmmmmmm!

-EDH

CHAPTER 2

Prayer

A revival may be expected when Christians have a spirit of prayer for revival. That is, when they pray as if their hearts were set upon it. When they go about groaning out their desire. When they have a real travail of souls

-Charles Finney

....

Every great movement of God can be traced to a kneeling figure.

-D.L Moody

....

In every book I have ever read on the subject of revival, prayer has alway been the largest section, and a theme that is repeated over and over again throughout the book. So, I make no apologies for a major emphasis on the topic of prayer in this little volume. If we have a desire and a longing in our heart for revival it begins, and it is sustained by prayer.

Just recently a pastor asked me, what percentage of revival came from God and what percentage came from man. "Ninety percent God" said I, "and ten percent man!" This may offend some and shock others. Look, salvation is all of grace and revival is all of God. However, as G. Campbell Morgan said, "Revival cannot be organized, but we can set our sails to catch the wind from heaven when God chooses to blow upon His people once again." Man has his responsibility, not

16

the least of which is prayer. Revival is not spasmodic; it's not like a mushroom that seems to just appear out of nowhere in the morning. Man must do his part and plead with God. Every revival that has been effective has been so because somebody had been praying.

Revival is the sovereign work of God, but that is not the main reason we do not see revival in our churches. The main reason is there are too few praying. Prayer is like the Cardiovascular system of the church, if the heart is weak, the body becomes sick. If the church is not praying, everything in the body is affected: the way we hear God, the way we experience God and the way we serve him. We need the arteries cleared from all the junk of the world and we need, need, need to seek God.

Ravenhill's words are beautiful, "Prayer is profoundly simple and simply profound. Prayer is the simplest form of speech that infant lips can try, and yet so sublime that it outranges all speech and exhausts man's vocabulary. A Niagara of burning words does not mean God is either impressed or moved. One of the most profound of Old Testament intercessors had no language — "Her lips moved, but no voice was heard." (1Samuel 1:13) No linguist here! There is "groaning which cannot be uttered."

I do not know of anything more needed in the church than revival, nor anything less sought after. We will pray for sister so and so's second cousin's dog more than we will pray for revival. But someone says, "We need more missionaries!" I tell you, The church revived will mobilize! "Holiness, we need to pursue holiness!" Ok, here is my answer, The church revived, lives sanctified lives! "We need to help the poor!" Listen, the church revived, hears needy cries! "We need more money!" I say, The church revived pays its tithe! "We need unity!" And, the church revived will harmonize! "We need stronger families." Agreed, the church revived rebuilds lives! "But don't we need more evangelism?" Yes, but, the church revived will evangelize! "I feel the devil has had his way far too long." And I say, the church revived, will the devil pulverize! "Ah, if we only had wisdom!" It's available, the church revived makes the simple wise!

It is clear that prayer and revival are inseparable. Prayer must always be based on the redemption. "Having therefore, brethren, boldness to enter into the holiest by the blood of Jesus." (Hebrews 10:19) Revival prayer, must always, be accompanied by consecration. The putting away of sin; a heart work of confession, contrition, repentance and pledging ourselves to God. "Search me, O God, and know my heart: try me, and know my thoughts: and see if there be any wicked way in me, and lead me in the way everlasting." (Psalm 139:23,24)

Duncan Campbell proclaimed, "If you want revival, get right with God. If you are not prepared to bring the 'last piece,' for God's sake, stop talking about revival, your praying is but the laughing-stock of the devils."

(More regarding this in chapter 9 on holiness.)

When praying for revival, we must always approach our gracious God with persistent faith. Faith that lays hold on God and does not let go until God shows up. As Calvin Colton wrote, "Revival never came to the church that did not believe it would come and revival never failed to come to the church that believed it would come."

John Wesley says, "Bear up the hands that hang down, by faith and prayer; support tottering knees. Have you any days of fasting and prayer? Storm the throne of grace and persevere therein, and mercy will come down."

Prayer for revival is in some ways very much like all other prayers.

1. "Ye have not because, ye ask not". (James 4:2). Why do we not have revival? Two possible reasons, God is sorely displeased with His church and will not send revival or, there is no one to stand in the gap. "And He saw that there was no man, and wondered that there was no intercessor... "(Isaiah 59:16) It is one thing to be denied revival, it far worse to go without because we did not take the time to ask. "...for as soon as Zion travailed, she brought forth children." (Isa 66:8") I hear someone say, "If there is revival to be had, I

would welcome it,... if it does not interfere with my sports or recreation." In other words, my Christian experience is not the greatest but it's livable. I endure but I do not enjoy! I will even give lip service to the need for revival, but, the truth be known, I'm not sure it will come and if it did come, I'm not sure it would fix anything." Meanwhile, Jesus is being wounded in the house of His friends. The world has heard the words, "Hitherto shalt thou come but no further" (Job 38:11) and they just laugh. They advance on Immanuel's land and defy the army of the living God and blaspheme His holy name. I ask you, is there not a cause? We must advance, soldier of the cross,... on your knees, soul travail, as a woman giving birth. This is what is needed. Labour, labour, labour in prayer and we shall have the victory. How many are actually praying for one?

2. But let him ask in faith. Nothing wavering. "For he that wavereth is like a wave of the sea driven with the wind and tossed. For let not that man think that he shall receive anything of the Lord." (James 1:6,7). To pray the prayer of faith means, to pray expecting the desired outcome. Noah built an ark on dry land because he believed God would make it rain, though it had not as yet ever rained. When we approach God for revival we must come prepared for a sovereign move of God. Eyes heavenward, minds set on Christ, and hearts prepared like soil plowed for seed. Faith is the prime ingredient to revival. But how many approach God and ask timidly (when and if they ask at all) because they are not sure revival is for them or they are so ignorant of it they simply are not sure on what ground they stand? "But" You say, "I believe God can do it, that is why I pray to Him." Faith is not believing He can bring revival, He can do anything, Faith is believing He will do it. John Bunyan told us in his classic allegory, Pilgrim's Progress, that Christian

escaped Doubting Castle with the key of promise. "For thus saith the high and lofty One that inhabiteth eternity, whose name is Holy; I dwell in the high and holy place, with him also that is of a contrite and humble spirit, to revive the spirit of the humble and to revive the heart of the contrite ones." (Isaiah 57:15) "... shall he find faith on the earth?" (Luke 18:8)

3. "Ye ask and receive not, because Ye ask amiss, that ye may consume it upon your lusts." (James 4:3). Revival is never for man's glory but must always be to the glory of almighty God. "The true man of God", writes Ravenhill, "is heartsick, grieved at the worldliness of the church... grieved at the toleration of sin in the church, grieved at the prayerlessness in the church. He is disturbed that the corporate prayer of the church no longer pulls down the strongholds of the devil."

So, someone asks, "What can I do to help usher in revival?" The first work, and the most important work, is to labour in prayer. The apostle said, "My little children of whom I TRAVAIL in birth again until Christ be formed in you..." (Gal 4:19). Failing here we fail everywhere. (Ravenhill) It is imperative that there be a season of travailing in prayer before revival comes, just as labour pains precede the birth of a new born baby.

There was once a man who had a daughter with a rare, life threatening, disease. As the child grew weaker and more lethargic, he contacted every physician he could think of for a possible cure. Then he heard of a doctor many miles away, in another town, who was an expert in curing this type of sickness. He hurried to the town, not once thinking about sleep or food or any comfort for himself, all he knew was, he needed to talk with the Doctor. When he arrived at the doctor's office he ran into one of the examining rooms, interrupted the doctor, fell to the floor and begged him to come and heal his daughter. That is how we approach God for revival.

The church is sick, she is cold, she is weak, she is in a deplorable condition. What is needed is for us to come to the Great Physician and beg for revival. Talitha Cumi! (See Mark 5:41) "Give me children or else I die." (Genesis 30:1) O the shriek from the barren woman, O what heart wrenching pain in her supplication, O what bitterness of soul. O, that the barren church would agonize, "Lord, Give me souls or else I die, give us revival lest we languish in soul sickness."

Charles Finney penned these words, "As I have said before, it is when people yearn for God's benefits with unutterable agony that they pray prayers that infallibly prevail with God. Those who feel less burdened with revival's urgency ask for it in words but never find the blessing. Yet when a church unites in prayer and comes to grip with the essentiality of revival, they never fail to have one. I don't believe a church has been turned away empty. Sincere accord in prayer regarding the need for revival will secure agreement in every essential area."

It was reported by D.M. McIntyre that, "Before the great revival in Gallneukirchen broke out, Martin Boos spent hours and days and often nights in lonely agonies of intercession. Afterwards, when he preached, his words were as a flame, and the hearts of the people as grass."

Prayer is the precursor to any revival. Now, I thoroughly enjoy my times of prayer: spontaneous prayer, family devotional prayer, corporate prayer, and closet prayer. However, I am willing to sorrowfully admit, I occasionally encounter times of weak, and dry prayers, stemming mostly from carnal distractions; it is a battle for concentration. I am ashamed of some of my prayer times, but, that is on the side of my speaking to God, I just need to trust and concentrate. The other side is, God not willing to listen to my prayers, which would be much worse. Why would he not listen? If I regard iniquity in my heart (Ps 66:18) What is between me and God? That question must be answered and rectified. Let us approach God and ask Him where we need to be made right . Obey, believe, repent and plead for revival.

There is something else we must consider before revival prayer. Zechariah declares something called the spirit of supplication (Zechariah 12:10) This is nothing new but something that is seldom or never taught, yet, Spurgeon mentions it, along with Finney, Edwards and others familiar with revival. What is it? Well, we know Jesus makes intercession for us. (Rom 8:34) Also, the Spirit helps us when we pray, the Spirit makes intercession with groaning and the Spirit makes intercession for the saint according to the will of God (See Rom 8:26,27) There is nothing more pathetic than to pray pretending for revival: fake urgency and fake tears are repulsive but when the Holy Spirit enables us with the spirit of prayer, it is a beautiful thing. Some of us can pray out in five minutes but when the spirit of prayer is on us time does not exist. This is how many prayed in days of old for revival for hours and sometimes all night long. If we are serious about revival, let us ask for power from on high to assist us in prayer and when we have it, then it is a sure sign of revival.

Andrew Murray the great preacher and revivalist of the nineteenth century from South Africa writes, "Prayer is reaching out after the unseen; fasting is letting go of all that is seen and temporal. Fasting helps express, deepen, confirm the resolution that we are ready to sacrifice anything, even ourselves to attain what we seek for the kingdom of God."

But what does fasting mean to you? To some it means putting away the cell phone or other electronic devices for a day, in some cases these should be discarded, they have become an idol. But fasting for the church of old was that of self denial, putting away all distractions, like food, pleasures, comforts, and being locked away with God. Fasting was a time of deep humbling, a time for sacrifice. Why, I have been to some churches in Canada where they cannot even make it through a one hour church service without taking a break. Many cannot even do without a coffee or other refreshments and have to bring them into the place of worship. I have heard of men and women in remote areas in Africa who wake up at four am and walk ten to fifteen miles to church through very rough terrain at the peril of wild animals and with blistering temperatures. Once they reach the church meeting they will praise and worship for hours, they will pray and then sit attentively through a two and a half hour sermon and then walk back home. We held meetings in the Philippines back in 2003. We saw the dear people come early in the morning to the meetings in sweltering heat. The women came with children on their backs and children by their side. They came and sat in bamboo churches ready to worship and to hear the message preached. I asked the pastor what is the order of service? he said, "Church sing, Hiltons sing, you preach, den church sing, den Hiltons sing, you preach, den church sing, Hiltons sing, you preach again, den we sing, pray and we go." We sometimes think we have done pretty good if we have endured a sermon that has gone five minutes past twelve. Fasting is all about God: His glory, His honour, His praise, His will, and nothing to do with us. This may be difficult in our present day narcissistic generation but it is necessary.

I hear someone say, "I have prayed, I have fasted, I have consecrated myself, I have begged God for revival and still there is nothing, not even a cloud the size of a man's fist." I feel your disappointment, I have done the same. There is still one thing left to do. Wait,... confidently, patiently wait. The old adage is true, "Rome was not built in a day." and a baby is nine months in its mother's womb before it is born. This is where faith is required and tested. Sometimes the hardest thing to do is wait. Jesus commanded the disciples, "... but tarry in the city of Jerusalem, until ye be endued with power from on high [the Holy Ghost]" (Luke 24:49). But we do not wait as someone waiting for a bus, neither did the disciples, no, we must still put our hearts into prayer, as they also did. Now, we are not waiting for His entrance on the scene as at Pentecost, but we are waiting for an outpouring of the Spirit of revival on the church. A preacher I talked with the other day told me, "he's not praying for revival." I answered, "You should be!" He said, "No, I am praying, 'We would be emptied of self and filled with God'". I listened and replied, " When that happens, that is revival."

Have You Prayed

Have you prayed all night, till the break of day,
And the morning light drove the dark away?
Did you linger there, till the morning dew,
In prevailing prayer, did you pray it through?

Did you pray till the answer came,
Did you pray in the Saviour's name?
Have you prayed all night till morning light,
Did you pray till the answer came?

Did you pray it through till the answer came?
There's a promise true for your faith to claim;
At the place of prayer Jesus waits for you;
Did you meet Him there, did you pray it through?

As the Master prayed In the garden alone,
Let your prayer be made to the Father's throne;
If you seek His will He will answer you;
Are you trusting still, have you prayed through?

- William C Poole. (1915)

The Prayer Meeting

The eminent revivalist preacher Leonard Ravenhill poignantly wrote, "The Cinderella of the church of today is the prayer meeting. This handmaid of the Lord is unloved and unwooed because she is not dripping with the pearls of intellectualism, nor glamorous with the skill of philosophy; neither is she enchanting with the tiara of psychology. She wears the homespuns of sincerity and humility and so is not afraid to kneel."

Henry Blackaby wrote, "All revival begins, and continues, in the prayer meeting. Some have also called prayer the "great fruit of revival." In times of revival, thousands may be found on their knees for hours, lifting up their heartfelt cries, with thanksgiving, to heaven."

I think most of our churches would do anything rather than pray wholeheartedly, without reserve, right down to the last bristle of the tail. It is easy to give, to send, to practise, and to decorate. Prayer is soul work and work it is. Revival costs but it is well worth it.

Pastor Bill McLeod had a deep seated desire to see revival in his church and in his city and he knew prayer was the only way he would ever get to see it, so, in the words of Pastor McLeod, "I began by emphasizing the Wednesday night prayer meeting. I would say things like this, Miss Sunday morning if you have to; miss Sunday evening if you must; but never miss the prayer meeting unless you are dead." People began to take this seriously and prayer meetings began to grow. Then revival followed.

My pastor calls our midweek prayer meeting, "Church unplugged". I think most prayer meetings are pretty much bear bones, nothing extravagant. Maybe that is why most of our prayer meetings will only have up to ten percent of the congregation. I know that some of our schedules will not permit our attendance, but I wonder, have we become a people who are so sensation oriented? We will fill a stadium to hear a really cool worship band, or a Christian comedian, or seminars on how to improve our finances and that's okay, but make no mistake about it, the prayer meeting is the engine that drives the church; how many cylinders are we firing on? If we could fill our churches for prayer meetings, unplugged, humbly seeking God, down and dirty, with importunity, praying for revival, we would have it. All effective revivals must be baptized in prayer. That is, by immersion not sprinkled!

The effectual fervent prayer of a righteous man availeth much. (James 5:16)

I Need A Little Time to Pray

I've got so much to do, today,
I need a little time to pray.
I don't know how I'll make it,
But Lord, I'm gonna take it,
I need a little time to pray.

Time to get my ducks all in a row.
Time to lighten up my heavy load.
No better time to start;
Put the horse before the cart.
I need a little time to pray.

Kneeling on the floor by your bed.
At the table fold your hands bow your head.
Prostrate on the ground;
Let me tell you what I've found.
I need a little time to pray.

When trouble comes a knocking at the door;
The devil tells you what he has in store.
No time to hesitate.
It's time to supplicate.
I need a little time to pray.

A sister comes, she's hurting and in tears;
A brother says, "Life's giving him the gears."
Tell the Lord their needs,
It's time to intercede.
I need a little time to pray.

- EDH

There's a Heaven to Gain
....

The old preacher stood there in the pulpit
The church house was empty almost:
His eyes filled with tears, his mind filled with memories,
Of not so long ago.

There's a heaven to gain, and a Hell to shun;
The way is still straight, there's a race to be run.
You can live as you please, but you must pay the cost;
And the highway to heaven still goes by the cross

- The Rochesters

CHAPTER 3

Preaching

reacher, with all thy getting, get unction. Brethren, we could well manage to be half as intellectual if we were twice as spiritual. A sermon born in the head reaches the head. A sermon born in the heart reaches the heart. A spiritual preacher will under God produce spiritually-minded people. Unction is not a gentle dove beating her wings against the bars outside of the preachers soul; rather she must be pursued and won. Unction cannot be learned, only earned in prayer.

-Leonard Ravenhill

The best way to revive a church is to build a fire in the pulpit.

-D L Moody

If someone were to ask me who my heroes are I would not reply by listing the elite athletes of today or actors of the silver screen or even men and women decorated for valour in war. No, my heroes are our pastors. I also love the church with a very deep love, with all its warts. However, since I have never yet been to a church that did not need revival (and being in itinerant ministry for over twenty five years, I have seen numerous) why do we not see it? It is not God's fault. Here are three reasons and there are of course many.

1. A narrow minded and fearful pastor.
2. A stale and stagnant board
3. A lazy and indifferent congregation.

If the fault can be found in any of these, in spite of my affection for the church, let them be laid at their feet. (Whitefield)

The apostle Paul writes, "...it pleased God by the foolishness of preaching to save them that believe." (1Corinthians 1:21b) Ah, here may lie the problem. Where are the preachers? We have multitudes of teachers, multitudes of sermon readers, multitudes of entertainers; we live in an age when an entire denomination could be started by an awesome worship band, with catchy tunes, clever lyrics and a dynamic presentation. But if we would have precious souls, give us preachers: bold preachers, yes, preachers foolish enough to declare man's greatest need, the gospel.

Some of our preachers have become experts in football, or golf, or fishing but are deficient in the gospel. It is a sad day when men and woman, boys and girls, rich and poor, high and low come and sit in the pews and hear an eloquent sermon on philosophy, or a sensational message on finances, or rationalistic discourse on discipleship, or they will sit and listen to the ear ticklings of a comedian or a singer who delicately woos them, but they do not hear the gospel. O! How many have sunk into hell, being churched, but have never heard, they MUST be born again.

Seriously.... If the pastor of the church, WILL NOT preach the gospel, then, for the love of God, let them vacate the pulpit and allow someone who will. Has not the church become a harvest field for souls?

I fear there is jubilation in hell at the close of some of our church services. When Sally sinner and Roger reprobate have sat through another service still unconverted and have been made to feel very comfortable in their sin. The preacher proclaims, "God bless you, be at peace." and if possible, all heaven just weeps.

O for more holy boldness, as S. Chadwick exclaims, "Truth without enthusiasm, morality without emotion, ritual without soul, are things Christ unsparingly condemned. Destitute of fire, they are nothing more than a godless philosophy, an ethical system and superstition."

A certain preacher had an occasion to meet with a notable actor. The preacher asked, "How is it that you are able to captivate the attention of your entire audience and play every string of their emotion, having only fiction as your instrument? While I, on-the-other-hand have the truth and my hearers are unresponsive?" The actor replied, "Because I present fiction as truth and you present truth as fiction." Hmmm!

> Dear Preacher,
> God has not called us to fill churches but populate heaven.
> God has not called us to diplomacy but to discipline.
> God has not called us to watch our retirement plan but to watch and pray.
> God has not called us to tickle the ear but to pierce the heart.
> God has not called us to pacify the sinner but to preach the gospel.
> God has not called us to flower-strewn pathways but to suffer for Jesus.
> God has not called us to a career, He has prepared us for a call.
> God has not called us to sensational sermons but to save sinners.
> God has not called us to cure insomnia but to wake the dead.
> God has not called us to retreat from sin, Satan or the world, but for revival.

Oswald Chambers stated it like this, "A preacher is one who has realized the call of God and is to use his every power to proclaim God's truth. God takes us out of our own ideas for our lives and we are "batter'd to shape and use," as the disciples were after Pentecost... Let God have perfect Liberty when you speak. Before God's message can liberate other souls, the liberation must be real in you. Gather your material, and set it alight when you speak."

I spoke to a preacher the other day and asked him how his message went on Sunday, he answered, "Everyone seemed to enjoy it." To which I replied, "That is not ALWAYS good." Neither should approval be our goal. The preacher is to have God's word on his lips and his only desire is to be a instrument fit for the Master's use. I would rather endure the rebuke of the lukewarm, carnal Christian for being too harsh, or too demonstrative, or too passionate than to look into the disappointed eyes of the saint who is painfully aware that I waffled on the gospel for fear of man. I'd rather offend the delicate sensitivities of every hearer than to have to meet with God in repentant prayer because I refused to do His bidding. "The fear of man bringeth a snare... "(Proverbs 29:25)

It is not sufficient enough to declare a truth and expect people to simply believe it. People need to be convinced. Are you not fed up, sick and tired and disgusted every time you hear of a young person in the church who has overdosed on drugs, or alcohol, or have ran off and got pregnant or shacked up with someone? Does it not bother you when one of the young men or women in your congregation attempts suicide? Well it does me! There is only one reason for this, and that is we have failed to convince them of the truth, that Jesus is the answer. This is only possible if we are not convinced ourselves, or, we do not care enough to convince them with our lip and our life. Better to get the least in our churches with conviction to preach, than to have the Doctor of theology preach without resolve and in unbelief.

Charles Spurgeon wrote this on preaching, "When I have shot, and spent all my gospel bullets, and still there is little effect among the hearers, I then get in the gun and shoot myself at them." Spurgeon was saying, when I have preached the gospel: Christ crucified, the blood redemption, grace abounding, and no one seems to respond, I plead with my whole heart, warning, beseeching men to be reconciled to God through Jesus Christ.

My dear brothers, my observation, as one, who is the least of all preachers, is: we must reach our people on two levels: 1. The understanding and 2. The affections. (Whitefield) We need light and heat. I have heard many sermons that have had ample amounts of light but there is no heat. The sermon is dry, and lifeless. It could be a documentary. Good, but it only reaches the brain and misses the heart. I have also heard other preachers, who deliver only heat. It reaches everyone on an emotional, fleshly level; there is lots of thunder but no rain; It could be a three point sermon on a Readers Digest poem. It tugs at the heart strings but does not teach; it tickles the ear but parks the brain. We must have a balance of light and heat if we hope to reach the whole man: spirit, soul and body.

Spurgeon said these pointed words, "Having no feeling himself, such a preacher creates none, and the people sit and listen while he keeps to dry, lifeless statements, until they come to value him for being "sound", and they themselves come to be sound, too; and need I not add, sound asleep."

Robert Murray M'Cheyne left the preacher with these words, and we would do well to heed them, "Get your text from God - Your thoughts, your words, from God... It is not great talents God blesses so much as great likeness to Jesus. A holy minister is an awful weapon in the hand of God. A word spoken by you when your conscience is clear, and your heart full of God's Spirit, is worth ten thousand words spoken in unbelief and sin."

Every sermon delivered must be preceded by a burden; an anguish of soul. No bible college or seminary can teach this, and it's not learned from human books. It can only be obtained by sweet communion with the blessed Holy Spirit. This anguish drives the preacher to the throne of grace as natural as the sea rushes to the shore, or as an injured child to its mother. When,... my dear brother, when, was the last time you approached the sacred desk with a burden?

If we are ever to expect revival we need to appeal to the throne of grace for a fresh anointing of God Spirit. "And He hath made my mouth like a sharp sword; in the shadow of His hand hath he hid me, and made me a polished shaft; in His quiver hath He hid me." (Isaiah 49:2). The preacher must be like a weapon in God's arsenal. "Whatever else you fail of," writes David Brainerd, "do not fail of the influence of the Holy Spirit; that is the only way you can handle the conscience of men."

Robert Murray M'Cheyne observes, "When you write with a dry pen, without any ink in it, no impression is made upon the paper. Now, ministers are pens, and the Spirit of God is the ink. Pray that the pen may be filled with that living ink,...that the Word may remain in your heart, known and read of all men,...that you may be sanctified through the truth.

"Pastors must repent!" Says Finney, "We, my brothers, must humble ourselves before God. To call the people to repent isn't enough. We must take the lead in repentance, calling the church to follow."

> Thus, I am like Eli,
> The subject of punishment for not rebuking sin:
> Whereas I should humbly confess sin
> And fly to the blood of Christ for pardon
> And peace.
> Give me, then, repentance, true brokenness,
> Lasting contrition,
> For these things thou wilt not despise
> In spite of my sin.
> - Puritan Prayer, (Valley of Vision)

We must intercede for our preachers. The great prayer revival of 1857 In New York City gathered thousands together to pray for

God's blessing on the church and the city and God turned mundane, dry preachers into great trumpeters of revival. Many threw away their notes and under the power of the Holy Spirit their words were like a hammer that breaks to shivers the hard hearts of the people.

Let me now take you, my dear reader, by the hand for a moment and lead you to the office of a man, He reads this text from I Corinthians 16:9, "For a great door and effectual is opened unto me, and there are many adversaries." He quietly whispers an Amen. I would like you to picture the frame of this man bowed down in deep distress, he is praying, he prays from the very depths of his soul, he seems to be in the very throws of conflict. He is your pastor, (if he is a preacher indeed) he feels the call to preach, and cries out, "Woe unto me; if I preach not the gospel." He is exceedingly grateful for the opportunity, but there are many adversaries. Who are they? 1. Self: he feels utterly unworthy to even walk the stairs to the pulpit. He feels the weight of his own corruption, his frailty, his inadequacy and feels unfit for the task. Then, if he preaches well, he worries about his pride, if he preaches poorly he feels he has let his Master and the congregation down. 2. His church: he knows he has only one master yet, he has many critics, the deacons have an expectation of populating the church, and they fear something said might scatter the flock. The members when pricked by the Word attack the messenger and rather than repent, they hurl insult back in his teeth. 3. Satan: if we had spiritual eyes we would see how entrenched the enemy is in our assemblies. Every time the preacher opens his mouth to deliver a truth, there is a distraction: the sound system, children crying, coughing spasms, slumber, and countless diversionary thoughts. Then there is the attack, not only on the message, but the preacher, "Do not say that", "You're a fool", "No one cares", "lighten up" etc. You ask, what can I do? Intercede for your pastor, tonight, if you have to, give up sleep, but intercede. Enter into the battle on his behalf and see what God will do.

Could you imagine meeting someone outside of the bank and they in frustration cry out, "I hate that bank. All they do is take my money. I never receive anything from them!" The question must be asked, how much have you invested? If the answer is nothing, then, why expect anything? Dear friends, your pastor (if he is a pastor indeed) has laboured before the Lord; has agonized in prayer; he has sought the Lord's heart, His pulse, His mind. How insubordinate to show such low regard and disrespect for the office and the message. If we would intercede; if we would invest through prayer in the service, we would show greater encouragement to the preacher and would walk away with the dividend of great blessing.

Spurgeon said, "Now is the time for victory: shall we lose it? This is the high tide that will float us over the bar; now let us put out the oars; let us pull by earnest prayer, crying for God the Spirit to fill the sails! Ye who love God, of every place and every denomination, wrestle for your ministers; pray for them; for why should not God even now [pour] out His Spirit? What is the reason why we are to be denied a Pentecostal season? Why not this hour, as one mighty band, fall down before Him and entreat Him, for His Son's sake, to revive His drooping church?"

God is raising up preachers, men who have given their lives for the gospel; they have counted the cost. Just as the great orator Joseph Parker suggests, "The man whose little sermon is "repent" sets himself against his age, and will for the time being be battered mercilessly by the age whose moral tone he challenges. There is but one end for such a man—'off with his head'! You had better not try to preach repentance until you have pledged your head to heaven." Send them Lord! Empower them! Bless them O Lord.

Someone says, "I thought you love the preacher." I do, dear reader, we live in a day and age when people will not endure sound doctrine. It would be wonderful if they would. It would make preaching easier, but God has not called us to ease. The "seeker sensitive" movement has created an era in Christian history where many of our preachers stand on the side of people and not on the side of God. William Booth the founder of the Salvation Army is quoted as saying, "I wish that every graduate from my training school, could be suspended by a rope over hell for twenty four hours! Then they could see what they were saving men from. I want a vision of heaven in my mind and the stench of hell in my nostrils as I go to preach the gospel." John Wesley the great revivalist and evangelist of the eighteenth century said, "Give me one hundred preachers who fear nothing but sin and desire nothing but God, and I care not whether they be clergymen or laymen, they alone will shake the gates of hell and set up the kingdom of Heaven on Earth."

My dear preacher friend, at the end of all things, when all is said and done, when we stand at the Great Tribunal, we will not be asked, if we have shown love by making people feel better about themselves, or if we have made people comfortable while still in their sin, or if we have shown kindness by glossing over the truth to soften the pain of their rebellion. In hell there will be multitudes who have been coddled to death while sitting in Christian churches. What will be asked is,.... What did you tell them about the gospel?

The under-shepherd [pastor] really only requires one skill,... the ability to obey the Chief Shepherd.

REVIVAL

We need a burden for lost souls, yes we do.
We need a hunger for the holy word of truth.
We need a zeal for holiness.
Take a stand for righteousness.
It's time the Holy Ghost of God break through.

We need a Holy Ghost revival in the Land.
It's time the church of God takes a stand.
It's time to share the word,
Share the gospel we have heard.
It's time to draw our line in the sand.

We need an earth shaking, heaven sent, Holy Ghost revival: amen.
We need a sin hating, devil chasing,
mountain moving power: my friend.
We need to get out of the pew,
Share the Gospel; the good news.
We need a moving of God's Spirit again.

- EDH

CHAPTER 4

The word of God

*he word of God is too sacred a thing, and preaching too
solemn a work, to be toyed and played with, as is the usage
of some, who make a sermon but a matter of wit and fine
oratory. If we mean to do good, we must come unto men's hearts, not in
word only, but with power. Satan moves not for a thousand quips and
wit-cracks of rhetoric. Draw therefore, this sword out of your scabbard,
and strike with its marked edge; this you will find the only way to pierce
your people's conscience and fetch blood of their sins.*

- William Gurnell

In every revival in Biblical history, Israel always returned to the
authority of God's law. We also conclude, if there is anything
less than a full-scaled returning to the truth as it is found in holy
scripture, there is no meaningful revival. There are some who are
waiting for a mystical force, or a feeling, or sensation or some sort
of excitement and they will call that revival but manifestations,
in and of themselves, account for nothing. Jesus said, "The flesh
profiteth nothing: the words that I speak unto you they are spirit,
and they are life." (John 6:63). We tend to be pragmatists at heart.
We have said, "If it's working why change it? A little compromise, a
little watering down, a little worldliness, a little toleration of sin and
presto, more people." I hear someone say, "What is wrong with that?
Is that not our goal?" No!,... everything is wrong with that!,—our

mandate is not to just gather people but to make disciples; save souls; make people of the Word,... "Teaching them to observe <u>all things</u> whatsoever I have commanded you:..." (Matthew 28:20) Jesus said there will be those who say, "We have eaten and drunk in thy presence, and thou hast taught in our streets." That is, many will say, "We were in the church house, we were good moral people, we were baptized, we carried our Bibles, we even took communion." But he shall say, "I tell you, I know you not whence are, depart from me, all ye workers of iniquity." (Luke 13:26) Dear reader, I could stand behind a thousand different pulpits. I could hold my Bible in my hand and raise it above my head in front of thousands of people, and ask, "Is this the Word of God?" I'd hear "Oh, yes! Oh yes! It is the Word of God!" but the real question is not, Is the Bible the Word of God?... The real question is, does it have supreme authority over your life?

There must be a tearing down in some of these worldly monumental churches. There has been tremendous error, and I'm not talking about eschatology, I'm not even talking about the mode of baptism. I'm talking about blatant gross sin; adulatory, fornication, alcoholism, homosexuality, pornography and flagrant opposition to the clear teaching of scripture. I'm talking about worldly generated, earth born sensationalism. Do we really think this is pleasing to God? Know ye not that the friendship of the world is enmity with God? (James 4:4) But how many pastors are longing, yearning, drooling for these mega media monstrosities that spew out the lust of the flesh, lust of the eyes and the pride of life. The apostle tells us, this is not of God but of the world. The world passeth away, and the lust thereof: but he who doeth the will of God abideth forever. (1John 2:17) All I know is this, the church that embraces worldliness, must, when revival comes throw these worldly ways overboard or no revival.

In most revivals of the past there were great numbers of people added to the church but I am thinking that a revival today, at least at the outset, would bring a blessed subtraction to many of our assemblies. A revival will always bring people back to the authority of scripture. I can hear many church goers saying, "This is not what I bargained for, I thought church was family, friends, fun and fellowship." How devastating for these to discover that church is a military training ground to battle against sin."

Spurgeon wrote, "If we want revivals, we must revive our reverence for the Word of God."

There is no revival until we wholeheartedly return to the Word of God. A great picture of a revived soul is drawn for us in Martha's sister, Mary, as she, "which sat at Jesus' feet, and heard His word." (Luke 10:39) Our goal is not to puff up our heads but to develop a deeper, intense adoration for our Lord and Saviour. That I may know Him,...(Philippians 3:10)

"Did not our hearts burn within us,... while He opened to us the scriptures?" (Luke 24:32).... In the state of revival the scriptures have a sizzling effect on the inmost part of our being: our icy hearts. This sovereign work occurs as the Spirit of God, accompanied by the Word of God, strikes, and fuses into the power of revival. When Peter preached at Pentecost it was the sovereign work of the Spirit of God accompanied with the Word of God, and "they were pricked in the heart." (Acts 2:37) The golden arrow of revival penetrated the most hardened of frozen hearts.

It was said of John Owen, the great Puritan preacher of the seventeenth century, during one of his sermons, that he impersonated God, saying, "You have profaned my word, you have disobeyed my word, you have left my Bible to gather dust. You shall no longer have my Bible. I will remove it from you." Then he impersonates the apostate person by falling to his knees, lifting his hands in the air, and with tears, cries, "No Lord take not thy Bible from me. Take my home, my crops, my children, but take not thy word." Funny isn't it? I think I would hear someone today say, "Take your Bible, but don't take my T.V. Take your inspired word but do not take my trinkets, and toys and other worldly pleasures.

"For the word of God is quick and powerful, and sharper than any two-edged sword, piercing even to the dividing asunder of soul and spirit, and joints and marrow, and is a discerner of the thoughts and intents of the heart. "(Hebrews. 4:12) Blessed weapon of God it both cuts and heals. It cuts the hard heart and heals the broken hearted.

Ephesians 6:17 describe the word thus, "... the sword of the Spirit which is the Word of God." Reader, we must slay sin in self. The nimble sins: they only show up now and then, usually at great spiritual victories or defeats, they are hard to catch, they move fast but they must be slain: selfishness, priggishness, arrogance, self-aggrandizement, petulance, etc. They are difficult to kill but they must die.

Then there are the sins like a cat. They seem to have nine lives or, although they have been thrust through they never seem to die. Take the sword of the Spirit which is the Word of God and slay them. Even if you do not kill them, wound them so they no longer have power over you. You know their names.

Then there are the little sins; they are small, they seem harmless and nobody notices them or cares about them but, they are like little children, they have a tendency to grow up. Kill them. They will cry, "Oh spare me, we are harmless." kill them or a little over-ambition can become a tyrant, a little nosiness will become gossip, a little desire will become theft and a little embellishment becomes blatant deception. Yes it is true we will alway have to deal with sin in this life but sin must never be a friend; it must always be hated as an enemy. If a little but hideous spider was seen crawling up your kitchen wall what would you do? Kill it! Go and do thou likewise.

Then there are the darling sins, the sweetheart sins: Saul was to kill all the Amalekites and destroy all they had but Saul kept back the best part. (See 1Samuel 15:15) We can be like that, we will slay pride but spare greed or we will kill hate but we will spare lust. Do you remember the great hero of the faith, Elijah, on mount Carmel, He challenged four hundred and fifty prophets of Baal. At the end of the great contest, after God sent fire from heaven and devoured the sacrifice of Elijah, the water and the stones, Elijah took a sword and he slew all the prophets of Baal. Let his cry be ours, "Let not one escape". (1Kings 18:40) Make no mistake about it, this is what revival looks like. It is letting the word of God and the God of the word have supremacy.

We must take the sword of the Spirit which is the Word of God and slay error in the church. Someone says, "Oh, we have a good pastor, one who trembles at God's word." I am so glad to hear that, but your pastor does not want you to park your brains. We must be as the Bereans, "... in that they received the word with readiness of mind, and searched the scriptures daily, whether those things were so." (Acts 17:11) We also should spiritually surround the sacred desk with flaming swords like the angels at Eden's gate and pray. Perhaps we need a rebuke from the word,... has the church become too worldly? Is there unforgiveness? May the Sword of the Spirit which is the Word of God have its free course in our churches, then only will we have revival.

Watch the songs we sing. There are many people who have formed their entire theology based on the songs they have heard. Are our songs true? What about the songs we hear during special music; soloists and quartets or guest singers. Is what they are singing true? Does it line up with scripture? Watch even our DVBS songs, are they telling the truth? It is just as sinful to sing a lie as to tell a lie. Children go home and sing these tunes because they are catchy. But are they true? A mother asks the child, "What is that you're singing sweetheart?" If what they are singing is untrue the unsaved parent is also being duped. The music has become a huge part of our services. May the Sword of the Spirit which is the Word of God have authority in our songs.

Then we must slay error in the world. But someone says, " What can we do, we are so small and so weak?" I think I see eleven men standing still, and I shout to them, "Hey what are you going to do now, your Master is dead!" Peter, their spokesman replies, "We shall preach the gospel to every creature."(Mark 16:15) "How are you going to do that," I say. "We have the Sword of the Spirit which is the Word of God and besides, Jesus said, "And lo I am with you always even to the end of the world." (Matthew 28:20) Did they not turn the world upside down? Where are the worshippers of Dianna, of Jupiter, of Baal and Ashtaroth? These idols are smashed to pieces. While It is true, in some cases, there seems to be a resurgence of the worshipping these idols, yet, they never will really recover except for a few isolated, unstable persons.

I see a lonely young monk, he has a hammer in his right hand, a nail between his lips and a paper in his left hand. It is October 31st 1517. Martin Luther is about to nail the ninety-fifth theses to the door of the church at Wittenberg which sparked the Protestant Reformation. Who is this I see, a small man bent over, working in his tinker shop. His name is John Bunyan, the famed writer of, "The Pilgrim's Progress". This is the second most read book in history, second only to the Bible. A book that has changed more lives than any other, non biblical book in history. I can see a young man clearing tables in the Bell Inn 1722. His name is George Whitefield and along with John Wesley and Johnathan Edwards and David Brainerd, the Great Awakening of 1741 was ushered in. I see a twelve year old boy working in the bowels of the earth as a coal miner. This boy will grow into a man and God will get a hold of his heart and at the age of twenty six Evan Roberts will lead the great Welsh Revival of 1904. Mr. Roberts once asked a friend, "Do you think it would be asking God too much for one hundred thousand souls?" God did not give Roberts one hundred thousand souls, no, God gave him one hundred and fifty thousand souls. I see two woman, Betty Smith, a blind woman of eighty four and her sister Christine whose body is wracked with arthritis. The year is 1949, they changed their little cottage into a sanctuary and they prayed for revival and God answered them with the most powerful revival in recent history, it was on the Isle of Lewis. Through God we shall do valiantly for it is He that shall tread down the enemy. The Sword of the Spirit is the Word of God.

What does the Bible say about itself in regard to revival? Well, let us look into sacred writ from the poet of Israel, "The law of the Lord is perfect, converting the soul: the testimony of the the Lord is sure, making wise the simple. The statutes of the Lord are right, rejoicing the heart; the commandment of the Lord is pure, enlightening the eyes. The fear of the Lord is clean, enduring forever: the judgements of the Lord are true and righteous altogether.

More to be desired are they than gold, yea, than much fine gold: sweeter also than honey and the honey comb. Moreover by them is thy servant warned: and in keeping of them there is great reward. Who can understand his errors? cleanse thou me from secret faults. Keep back thy servant also from presumptuous sins; LET THEM NOT HAVE DOMINION OVER ME;...." (Psalms 19:7-13)

Also a great study on the word and revival is found in Psalm 119 where the Psalmist admonishes us through the Holy Spirit, v.25 "...quicken" (or the same word, revive) "thou me according to thy word." v.37 "...quicken thou me in thy way." v.40 "Behold, I have longed after thy precepts: quicken me in thy righteousness." v.88 "Quicken me after thy loving kindness; so shall I keep the testimony of thy mouth." v.107 "I am afflicted very much: quicken me, O Lord according to thy word." v.149 "....O Lord quicken me according to thy judgements." v.159 "Consider how I love thy precepts: quicken me, O Lord, according to thy loving kindness." Revival and the word of God are inseparable . It's revival but its revival God's way, in His time, in His appointed place, for His glory.

The Spirit of God in conjunction with the Word of God

We have read, "The word of God is quick and powerful..." (Hebrew 4:12) We have also read, "the gospel is the power of God..." (Roman 1:16) Is dynamite powerful? "Oh yes" you say, "dynamite is very powerful." But wait just a minute, if I took a stick of dynamite and threw at you what would happen? Nothing, Why? What is needed? A wick and a fuse. Likewise, every cult, every "ite" and "ism" has the same Word of God but they do not have the Spirit of God. The Word of God is the dynamite and the fuse is the Spirit of God. Paul said, "And my speech and my preaching was not with enticing words of man's wisdom, but in a demonstration of the Spirit and power." (1Corinthians 2:4) There must be a total reliance on both, or better said, on the two as one, the Sword of the Spirit which is the Word of God. We can only approach revival based on the absolute assurance of the power and veracity of scripture.

Titus Conan, evangelist and missionary of the 1800"s reported, During The Hawaiian Revival 1836 The Hilo church adopted the Bible as its "Confession of Faith". When individuals became members of the church, they placed their hand on the Bible and promised "to abstain from all that is forbidden and to obey all that is written therein." The missionaries also urged church members to abstain from use of tobacco and alcohol. Many natives struggled to break addictions to these substances, yet during the revival, multitudes pulled up all their tobacco plants and cast them into the sea or into pits and thousands of pipes were broken upon rocks or burned, and thousands of habitual smokers abandoned the habit at once, forever."

-Elmer Towns and Douglas Porter (The Ten Greatest Revivals Ever)

HOLY SPIRIT LIGHT DIVINE

Holy Spirit, Light divine, shine upon this heart of mine.
Chase the shades of night away;
turn my darkness into day.
Holy Spirit, Power divine,
cleanse this guilty heart of mine.

Long hath sin without control
held dominion o'er my soul.
Holy Spirit, Joy divine, cheer this saddened heart mine.
Bid my many woes depart;
heal my wounded, bleeding heart.
Holy Spirit, all divine, dwell within this heart of mine.
Cast down every idol throne;
Reign supreme, and reign alone.

-Andrew Reed. (1871)

SPIRIT OF THE LIVING GOD

Spirit of the living God, fall fresh on me,
Spirit of the living God, fall fresh on me,
Melt me, mold me, fill me, use me.
Spirit of the living God fall fresh on me.

-Daniel Iverson (1926)

CHAPTER 5

The Holy Spirit

O h for a great and general revival...Let us pray for such a
visitation of the Holy Ghost with our whole souls. It is not
only desirable, it is essential; we must either be revived by the
Lord Himself, or the church will descend until error and ungodliness
swallow them up. This calamity shall not happen but only divine grace
can avert it.

- C.H. Spurgeon

We preachers love to quote Spurgeon the silver tongued, prince
of preachers, but let us ponder the solemnity of these words as he
exhorts his hearers on revival. "Death and condemnation to a church
that is not yearning after the Spirit, and crying and groaning until
the Spirit has wrought mightily in their midst." I can hear the cry
for more money in some of our churches, more activities, or better
worship but what we need is a cry for the Spirit being poured out in
revival. If what Mr. Spurgeon said is true, then I believe we have the
answer to our dead churches, there is no travail for the Spirit of God.
Let us pray like Isaiah, "Oh that thou wouldest rend the heavens,
that thou wouldest come down,..." (Isaiah 64:1)

There may be some reading who are thinking, "here is where we
will talk about the gifts of the Spirit." Emphatically yes! The gift of
repentance, through the Holy Spirit. (See 2Timothy 2:25) In every
bona fide revival God's Spirit was poured out and there was genuine

brokenness. In the Welsh revival the cry was, "Arglwydd phlygu i mi" "O Lord bend us" but it was spoken in the Welsh tongue and has far greater meaning in Welsh than in English. Dr. Orr states, "Everything that went into the chorus: Melt me, Mold me, Fill me, Use me, would go into that word "bend". Bend means "to shape" like shaping clay on a wheel. Evan Roberts prayed in great agony, "bend us."

"Why not the sign gifts? Cannot God still do signs and wonders?" He can do whatever He wants. But the apostle Paul wrote, "For I determined not to know anything among you save Jesus Christ and Him crucified." (1Corinthians 2:2) The overarching theme of the apostle Paul's ministry was Jesus Christ and Him crucified! But why? He was a brilliant man endowed with the Spirit, and could unlock deep mysteries found in scripture, and this he did, but it wasn't his primary call. He was used by the Lord to bring divine healing and he even raised the dead. No doubt this could have attracted vast numbers of people, and I'm sure it did. He was a persuasive teacher and was able to instruct how we must live, and this he included in each of his epistles. Paul was fully aware that a person could have knowledge but be lost, they could receive a miracle and still perish and they could live an upright, moral life and still burn in hell. On the other hand let he/she come to the cross as a sinner, believing on the all sufficient merits of Christ, both doing and suffering all that was required for their salvation and they have the one thing needed.

I am grieved over those who have alleged gifts of the Spirit but they lack the fruit of the Spirit. I have never experienced a fraction of what others say they have, but I have the Bible which is a more sure word of prophecy. I would like inscribed on my gravestone these words, "I did no miracle: but all things that I spake of this man Jesus were true and many believed on Him there." (See John 10:41,42)

The Holy Spirit is the great teacher, He is called the Spirit of Truth, therefore all that is error is made suspect by Him as He checks our spirit. Think of the times when you felt something amiss, you listened to something presented as truth but there was an awareness that what was said or sung was wrong, or unscriptural but it was treated as nothing. In the process of time, as this happened on a continual basis, the Holy Spirit stops prompting. It matters little to you if things do not line up with scripture, if it feels good, or if everyone else likes it, you swallow it. But during revival there is an awakening, a resurgence of the Holy Spirit in our hearts. We are "reproved" and no longer does a man-centred gospel attract but rather it repels. When we hear another man-centred message it become loathsome to us, we esteem it as much good as another truck load of sand dumped in the desert. Our hearts now long for Jesus, water for the thirsty soul. He, the Holy Spirit, will glorify me, said Jesus (John 16:14).

Yes, Jesus Himself taught us, "He [the Holy Spirit] shall glorify Me" (John 16:14) When we pray for revival we are not praying for a passion for souls or for reclaiming of prodigals, that is the effect, we need a passion for Jesus. Jesus has a passion for the lost. We do not pray the effect we pray the cause. If we are praying by the Spirit, we will glorify Jesus. This needs to be an all encompassing burden. Jesus said, "And I, if I be lifted up from the earth, will draw all men unto me. (John 12:32)

The apostle John was in the Spirit on the Lord's day (Revelation.1:9) hence the Revelation. Revelation is the supernatural ability of the Holy Spirit to make the unseen reality. He impresses upon us the reality of where true value lies. The sin of Adam was that he embraced that which was seen and temporal at the expense of that which was unseen and eternal. The Holy Spirit in times of revival takes that which is dim and cloudy because of the lust of the flesh, the lust of the eyes and the pride of life and makes it a brilliant revelation. No longer is popularity important, only Christ's approval. No longer is prosperity essential, only riches in Christ. No longer do possessions identify us, we need only to be possessed by Christ. Jesus becomes more real than this book you are reading, more real than the person writing it, more real than anything or anyone. This is the Holy Spirit's work in revival!

The Holy Spirit is the most misunderstood member of the Trinity. In times of revival it is He who is often blamed for the manifestations of mere enthusiasts. Do not get me wrong when someone is burnt there is a reaction; when someone is zapped with an electrical shock there is a reaction. Likewise when the Holy Spirit is poured out in times of revival there will be a reaction. I have heard the cries of men and women desiring from the depths of their heart, "cleanse me". I have seen weeping on altars: men and women, young and old, rich and poor in the bitterness of their souls. But there are other reactions that make our Lord the Holy Spirit look like a fool. This grieves Him and in some cases amounts to borderline blasphemy. It would, however, be foolishness to toss out the gold because there is ore mixed with it, but let us rather, refine it by seeking the fire of the Spirit of truth.

Spurgeon accurately observes that, "the church will never prosper until more reverently it believes in the Holy Ghost. He is so good and kind, that it is sad indeed that He should be grieved by slights and negligence."

And when He (the Holy Spirit) shall come, He will reprove the world of sin..." (John 16:8) There have been many, who have been convinced of sin by sound logic. Many who have been awakened to sin by a forceful argument. But O that more would be reproved, or another way of saying it, convicted by the Holy Spirit. Conviction, in the real sense of the word, will lead to one of two ultimate conclusions: one, total despair, the other, the cross of Jesus Christ. (Chambers)

Robert Murray M'Cheyne the young revivalist preacher of 1835 to 1843 wrote this, "Even He (the Holy Spirit) all wise, almighty, all gentle and loving though He be, cannot persuade a poor sinful heart to embrace the Saviour, without first opening up his wound, and convincing him he is lost.

Now, brethren, I ask you, Should not the faithful minister of Christ just do the very same? Ah! brethren, if the Spirit, whose very breath is all gentleness and love - whom Jesus hath sent into the world to bring men to eternal life - if he begins his work in every soul that is saved by convincing of sin, why should you blame the minister of Christ if he begins in the very same way?"

My dear reader, there is nothing more disturbing than a Christless Christianity and a spiritual experience devoid of the Holy Spirit. But I fear this is becoming the new normal in many of our churches. Christless Christianity is like a Christmas tree, it looks pretty but it is dead, and much of what is seen is nothing but cheap ornaments of piety, good deeds, much energy and outward morality, but it is Christless. (Nicholson) Spirituality without the Holy Spirit is what is desperately conjured up in some of our church services until we feel something, but goosebumps, and tingles are poor substitutes for the genuine thing. I think the devil himself could care less about our little religious experiences, little excitements, and holy chills because he knows these pose no threat to his kingdom, he knows most will be just like before, dead and cold and dishonouring to the Master.

David Brainerd said, "Whatever else you fail of, do not fail of the Holy Spirit; that is the only way you can handle the conscience of men."

The Moravian Revival

Such was the thirteenth of August, seventeen hundred and twenty-seven. Count Zinzendorf, the one outstanding human leader and spokesman, called it "the day of the outpouring of the Holy Spirit upon the congregation,—it's Pentecost". Again he described it as follows: "The Saviour permitted to come upon us a Spirit of whom we had hitherto not had any experience or knowledge. Hitherto had been leaders and helpers. Now the Holy Spirit Himself took full control of everything and everybody."

After the Holy Spirit had been poured out on the Berthelsdorf Church, a great hunger for the Word made it necessary for additional meetings. The church services were increased to three times,... that is, three times a day, every day of the week: five am, seven am, and nine pm. It was also determined that there should be increased prayer. So they began a prayer meeting. The prayer meeting was divided into twenty-four, one hour segments, each hour being filled every day. This prayer meeting was sustained, unabated, every day, three hundred and sixty five days a year and lasted one hundred years.

The revival in Herrnhut gave the men and woman, of the church, a heart like Jesus for a lost world. After hearing a testimony from an escaped African slave from the West Indies island of St.Thomas, two men felt God calling them to go there and preach the gospel. There was an estimated five thousand slaves on the Islands and there was an aversion by the plantation owners towards anything to do with Christianity. So Leonard Dober and David Nitschmann sold themselves into slavery to reach these precious souls for Jesus. With no hope of ever returning the young missionaries went, and as the ship pulled away they cried out to their loved ones, "May the Lamb who was slain, receive the reward of His suffering."

COME HOLY SPIRIT

Come, Holy Spirit, I need you
Come, sweet Spirit, I pray
Come in your strength and your power
Come in your own special way.

- Heritage Singers

O BLESSED HOLY SPIRIT

O blessed Holy Spirit, illuminate my mind,
Breath upon the Scripture that Jesus I shall find.
O descend upon my being, like a gentle Dove,
And open up my dim eyes, that I behold His love.

O blessed Holy Spirit, my comfort so sublime.
Tell me once again of unseen truths divine.
Open up my heart; pour in the oil and wine.
That Thy word shall heal all that sin has grimed.

O blessed Holy Spirit, pour salve upon mine eyes,
That I see Jesus only for my pardon He devised.
Just to look upon those wounds a wonder to behold
That the cure for sin and shame may ever be retold.

O blessed Holy Spirit, Thou sweet sanctifying One,
My life I now surrender to what the cross has done.
My life, my soul, my heart, all that Thou desire
I make myself an offering that I might lift Thee higher.

O blessed Holy Spirit, revival's what I require,
That I would magnify the Saviour, and be a holy fire.
Arouse my dreary, sleeping soul, melt my icy heart,
Make me what I ought to be, to You I am set apart.

- EDH

CHAPTER 6

Worship

evived souls never need to be told how or why they worship. The Holy Spirit has fanned the dim embers of apathy into vibrant flames of devotion; they cannot help but worship in spirit and in truth.

- EDH

Much time, money and effort goes into the singing portion of our worship services. Worship leaders work hard to improve our lacklustre praises: better multimedia presentations, better platform displays, better equipment, better talent, etc. I would say, let us strive for excellence. However, I would also say, ho hum praise and worship is an indication of a deeper problem. While there is no sin in our musical improvements, we must keep in mind, the latest and greatest is not revival. And, while poor participation in our singing is an indicator of the need for revival, vibrant worship is not an indication there is no need. Perception is not always reality. Outward performance is often times just outward performance. I fear in many ways we have not been too far removed from Roman Catholicism. I know we do not swing the incense, we do not do the chants, we do not robe our priest but the concept is the same. It is sensational worship; the idea of creating a religious experience devoid of God. Keep in mind, God's ear is not tuned to great talent and His heart is not moved by great productions but by a great likeness to Jesus.

It is said, God inhabits the praises of His people, but it would seem, the devil inhabits some of our worship teams. It is often here where there is disharmony, disunity, and discontentment. It is also here where the most despicable part of his malignant nature is displayed, pride. (No surprise, since God so loves our praises, that the devil should hate it.) The Bible teaches, Hosea 10:11 "Judah shall plough" I take that to mean: Judah, whose name means, "praised", shall prepare the soil. The worship team is in place to lead the church in holy praise and worship to our exalted Lord, and also, for preparation of the soil of ones heart for the seed of the word. However, I have also seen where some worship teams have led the church into worldliness. Is it not here where personal self image is showcased?... where improprieties are observed?... and where rebellion is seen as a virtue? Great talent, without holiness, humility and authenticity is repulsive to God and a snare to the church!

My pastor shared this thought in a message he preached about worship. He quoted this from, Christianity Today, in an article by John Ortberg and Pam Howell. "'God is Spirit, and they that worship Him must worship Him in spirit and in truth.' (John 4:24) There are two major errors which the church needs to avoid when it comes to worship. The one is the enthusiastic, energetic and sensational type of worship; every song being presented solely on an emotional level. This worship is often shallow, sometimes artificial and rarely reflective. Little attention is given to worshipping with the mind. This is Scarecrow worship: it would be better if it only had a brain. The second is worship focussed on biblical correctness and emphasizes theological truths. They can recite their creed and cannot tolerate error, they carefully craft their prayers but if the truth be known they are bored. There is no wonder and no passion. This is Tin Man worship: it would be better if it only had a heart." Blessed is the church that worships in spirit and in truth, they have balance, they are true worshippers.

There is something for the born again Christian in their worship, that no one else can receive. However, I believe there is something for the revived Christian that other believers do not experience, but it is available to all who call on Jesus' name. When it is experienced, there is an inexpressible wonder to behold, this produces a preoccupation with God. This is deep, affectionate, filial worship. It is worship in spirit and in truth. Those who have enjoyed times like these are often misunderstood. It is a sweet intimacy with Christ and in times of revival it is not man reaching out to God but God initiating intimacy with man. God does rend the heavens and comes down; no longer are the heavens like brass. In times of this kind of intimacy, there is often an overwhelming feeling of uncleanness because of our infidelity. Beware of trying to create or recreate an intimacy like this, but without God. This is often tried but is never successful and is ugly.

The word "Phoney" has no place in the Christian experience. Yet the plastic, disingenuous, replica of Christianity has been easily detected by far too many unbelievers. Many have seen it and will never again return to the church. They accept it in business, in entertainment, in politics, in sports, even in relationships but it is not tolerated in the arena of the divine. Neither should it be tolerated in us.

> There can be no phoniness in our profession!
> There can be no phoniness in our worship!
> There can be no phoniness in our preaching!
> There can be no phoniness in our witness!
> There can be no phoniness in our prayers!
> There can be no phoniness in our giving!
> There can be no phoniness in our adoration of Jesus!

There was nothing of the sort in Jesus; let revival banish it far from us. David said, "Then shalt thou be pleased with the sacrifices of righteousness..." (Psalm 51:19)

TAKE MY LIFE

Take my life, and let it be
Consecrated, Lord, to thee;
Take my hands, and let them move
At the impulse of Thy love;
At the impulse of Thy love.
Take my feet, and let them be
Swift and beautiful for Thee.
Take my voice, and let me sing
Always, only, for my King;
Always, only, for my King.

Take my lips, and let them be
Filled with messages for Thee.
Take my silver and my gold:
Not a mite would I withhold:
Not a mite would I withhold.

Take my will, and make it Thine,
It shall be no longer mine;
Take my heart, it is Thine own,
It shall be Thy royal throne.
It shall be Thy royal throne

Take my love, my Lord, I pour
At Thy feet it's treasure store;
Take myself, and I will be,
Ever, only, all for Thee.
Ever, only, all for Thee.

- Frances R. Havergal. (1874)

CHAPTER 7

Joy

A genuine revival without joy in the Lord is as impossible as spring without flowers, or a day-dawn without light.
-C.H. Spurgeon

"Wilt Thou not revive us again: that thy people may rejoice in Thee." (Psalm 85:7) It is no surprise the psalmist joins, revival and joy in the Lord, hand in hand. The unconverted has no capacity for authentic biblical joy. He may be happy but his happiness is transitory. Something new brings great happiness but the moment it is damaged, or it loses its lustre, happiness is quickly vanquished. Success can bring a delightful happiness but failure the next minute brings a dolorous sorrow. The believer has the potential for joy but it is still not automatic. In fact, I would say, it is quite pathetic to see the lack of joy on many Christians. But a revived soul is one who knows by experience, the joy of the Lord: it is supernatural: it is God's joy and is not subject to circumstance. If we would desire, as Peter writes, "Joy unspeakable and full of glory" (1 Peter 1:8), let us seek revival.

For the joy of the Lord is your strength. (Nehemiah . 8:10) This joy, the world did not give us and the world cannot take it away. But dear friends, we can give it away, or allow it to be stolen. Where is your joy metre at? If it's running very low, check where there has been compromise, and there you will find the place you squandered your precious gift, repent, and it will return. Or perhaps, you have been visited by the joy thieves, their names are: Mr. Discouragement, Mr. Doubt, Mr. Negative, Mr. Envy and Giant Despair. These have no right to your supply of joy, but you have left the door of your heart unattended. So remove the sword of the Spirit from its scabbard and cut them to pieces. Then watch God replenish that which the thief has stolen for, has killed for, and destroyed for and your abundant life will be restored.

We would expect joy in heaven, no more pain, no more sickness and every tear will be wiped from our eyes. In heaven there will be streets of gold, the crystal sea, gates of pearl, walls of jasper; scenes too brilliant for mortal language to describe, but this is not why we will have joy, we will have joy because we will be in the presence of Jesus Christ, the Lamb of God who took away our sin. Revival is not the bliss of heaven, we will enjoy after death, but it is as close to heaven as can be had on earth. "In thy presence is fullness of joy; at thy right hand there are pleasures for evermore." (Psalm16:11) This is for the here and now.

David declares, "Restore unto me the joy of thy salvation...." (Psalm 51:12) Some people respond to revival like those flies that appear dead in the window, and when a warm sun beams through the glass the flies come to life, that is, until it cools down again. (Spurgeon) Why?.... because there is a lack of surrender. God is in the restoration business. To restore is different than upgrading or revitalizing; restoring is: to completely strip down, right down to scruple. Then He puts us back, by the book, and claims every part for Himself. We can experience joy in our Christian walk but we will never experience the joy of His salvation until we have been restored. This is true revival.

Jonathan Edwards, the great American theologian of the eighteenth century, writes this of David Brainerd, the incomparable missionary to the Indigenous people of North Eastern United States. This he writes while Brainerd lay on his deathbed, suffering from the throws of consumption, in the Edward's home.

Journal entry Sept 27ᵗʰ 1747 "Early this morning, as one of the family came into the room, Brainerd expressed himself thus, 'I have had more pleasure this morning than all the drunkards in the world enjoy.' So much did he esteem the joy of faith above all the pleasure of sin."

My dear reader, God has promised abundant life. It is a promise found in the gospel of John 10:10 "The thief cometh not but for to steal, kill and destroy but I have come that ye might have life and that more abundantly." There are those who teach that God wants us wealthy, and healthy and there we will find such joy and contentment. Emphatically No! This is the world's joy, it is all they have. Real joy is not found in get, gather, gain and keep but in a deep, intimate relationship with Jesus. Real biblical Joy rises above our circumstances. Joy is what the Christian feels while languishing in a stinking prison for their faith in Jesus, like Paul and Silas. They sang a sonnet of praise to God at midnight while fettered with chains. Christian joy is what is experienced even though all earthly possessions are lost. They delight themselves in the Lord and offer the sacrifice of praise, saying, "What have I ever done to deserve even one of the blessings you give." This you will seldom ever hear from the lifestyles of the rich and famous. Joy is a Christian's blessing felt even at the loss of loved ones. No one would try to minimize the excruciating grief experienced at the death of a friend, or family member but there rises up in the heart inexplicable joy when hearing, "Precious in the sight of the Lord is the death of His saints". (Psalm 116:15) Joy is what is felt even on our own death bed. O, the rapturous hope of future prospects from God in heaven.... "Yea though I walk through the valley of the shadow of death, I will fear no evil: for thou art with me; thy rod and thy staff they comfort me." (Psalm 23:4) Real joy rises above, pain, poverty, perils and passing, and this is what is meant by those wonderful words, "Wilt thou not revive us again; that thy people may rejoice in thee." (Psalm 85:7) "In thy presence is fullness of joy; at thy right hand are pleasures for evermore." (Psalm 16:11) "Weeping may endure for the night, but joy cometh in the morning." (Psalm 30:5)

Welsh Revival 1859

All appeared to be baptized with the Holy Ghost and with fire. The meetings wore a solemn and calm aspect throughout. Many tears fell and many sighs rose up to heaven. The Lord owned His Word as His own, and the divine presence seemed to move through the mighty multitude... The cloud appeared to hang overhead behind and before us, and now and then a rich drop descended, but this afternoon the cloud burst and the shower fell, and the whole house of prayer was the habitation of joy. The heaven was so near the earth, that we seemed uncertain whether we were in the body or out of it.

Listen barren church, "The wilderness and the solitary place shall be glad for them; and the desert shall rejoice and blossom as the rose." (Isaiah . 35:1)

PICTURE ME

Picture me without Jesus and you'll see an a wasted life,
A heart filled with sorrow; a world filled with strife.
Like a ship without a rudder, A lock without a key;
A life without purpose, a soul in misery.

Picture me without Jesus and you'll see an empty heart,
A life wrecked, and ruined, a world torn a part.
Like a rose without a fragrance, a bird without a song;
A life without meaning, a world that's gone wrong.

But, I know He lives within my heart, His
promise, "never to forsake". (Heb. 13:5)
He's filled the empty void, where once there was an ache.
View a portrait of peace and joy, since Jesus took control.
He's painting His image on the canvas of my soul.

- EDH

CHAPTER 8

Unity

here is a growing conviction everywhere, and especially among thoughtful people, that unless revival comes, other forces will take the field, that will sink us still deeper into the mire of humanism and materialism.

-Duncan Campbell

Most times unity and tolerance are the words associated with peace among the brethren. And this can simply be accomplished by holding hands and singing songs to Jesus. But God joins peace with holiness, "Follow peace with all men and holiness..." (Hebrews 12:14) Unity can never be obtained apart from sound biblical doctrine. We must never endeavour for the lowest common denominator, that spells compromise and results in no intimacy with God and no revival. Better to be isolated and stand by the truth than to be unified by a lie and hypocrisy. We must press toward a full scale turning to God and His word. It is then that God pours out a blessing of real, authentic revival. "... they lifted up their voice to God with one accord,... and when they had prayed, the place was shaken where they were assembled together and they were all filled with the Holy Ghost, and they spake the word of God with boldness." (Acts 4:27 and v32) There is something about authentic biblical unity and powerful prevailing prayer that brings a metamorphosis on two accounts: 1. they were filled with the Holy Ghost which produced a boldness to speak the word of God, and, 2. the caravans of Hell trembled and the "place was shaken". What are we afraid of?... are we afraid a holy boldness will make us appear flakey, or are we afraid that the church foundation will not endure a hell shaking tremor?

A.T. Pierson wrote, "From the day of Pentecost, there has not been one great spiritual awakening in any land which has not begun in a union of prayer, though only among two or three; no such outward, upward movement has continued after such prayer meetings have declined."

It's appalling to see the state of many of our churches, brother is angry with brother, sister fighting with sister. Appalling! If God had only told us once in scripture that we should forgive or love one another that would be enough. But I can think off the top of my head, twenty verses, and I am sure there are many more. Recently, we visited a town and we calculated there were over one thousand churches within a sixty mile radius. Someone says, "Wow, how very spiritual that location must be." Most of these churches were established because people could not get along, and churches were split and then split again and so forth. This grieves the Holy Spirit; make no mistake about it, if any of us are harbouring bitterness we need to repent, and make it right, and we must do it now, or please do not call yourself a Christian, because it is a contradiction. God hates bickering, just as any parent hates it when their children are constantly quarrelling. Here is one reason why revival delays.

We in the church have given the devil a foothold. Yes, when we have shown ourselves to be the same, or worse than the world, we give cause for the unbeliever to look upon the church, with disdain and say, "See,... so much for your Christianity; you are no better than us." This is a deplorable truth in the area of unforgiveness. We need to be different from the world. Especially, since we are admonished by holy scripture, "And be ye kind one to another, tender hearted, forgiving one another, even as God for Christ's sake hath forgiven you." (Ephesians . 4:32). It was reported by Bill McLeod, the pastor of the church during the revival in Saskatoon in 1971, he stated, "...that Christians were challenged to reconcile fractured relationships. As they did so, revival came to the church and quickly spread throughout the community. A week of meetings turned into two months of revival services." Prayer for revival (or anything) must be preceded by forgiveness and reconciliation or forget it.

Saskatoon Revival 1971

During the Saskatoon revival in 1971 the chief of police in Saskatoon issued a report to the daily paper and said this, "I am not a religious person but I do know the difference between ordinary church work and revival. Revival has come to our city because we are having people coming to us and confessing crimes."

-Elmer Towns and Douglas Porter The Ten Greatest Revivals Ever

Weeds grow naturally in the earth because weeds are indigenous to it. We never have to be trained in the art of murmuring, complaining, strife or unforgiveness because they are natural to our earthly nature. To live at peace we must live above our earthly nature. "Seek those things which are above... Set your affections on things above, not on things of earth." (Colossians 3:1,2)

> Two natures beat within my breast,
> The one is cursed, the one is blessed,
> The one I love, I one I hate.
> The one I feed will dominate.
> Author unknown

D.L. Moody writes, "See how He came on the day of Pentecost! It is not carnal to pray that He may come again and that the place may be shaken. I believe Pentecost was but a specimen day. I think the Church has made this woeful mistake that Pentecost was a miracle never to be repeated. I have thought too that Pentecost was a miracle that is not to be repeated. I believe now if we looked on Pentecost as a specimen day and began to pray, we should have the old fire here in Boston."

Dear reader, take warning: the bitter venom of pride is death to any revival, or hope of revival, because it is fatal to genuine unity, but, "Behold, how good and how pleasant it is for brethren to dwell together in unity." (Psalms 133:1) To our Heavenly Father there is a placidness that comes when His children are in one accord. It is during these times when He pours out a blessing on the church. "And when the day of Pentecost was fully come, they were all with one accord in one place. And suddenly there came a sound from heaven as of a mighty rushing wind, and filled the house where they were sitting." (Acts 2:1,2) If we are to experience the power of God or a move of God or the fullness of God, we must humble ourselves and unify around the Word of God for one purpose, that Jesus be lifted up. "And I, if I be lifted up from the earth, will draw all men unto me." (John 12:32)

Rise up, O church of God!
Have done with lesser things.
Give heart and mind and soul and strength
To serve the King of Kings.

- William P. Merrill 1911

CHAPTER 9

Holiness

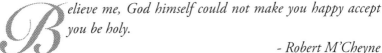

elieve me, God himself could not make you happy accept you be holy.

- *Robert M'Cheyne*

All true revival is ever related to holiness.

- *Duncan Campbell*

"Follow peace with all men, and holiness, without which no man shall see the Lord." (Hebrews. 12:14) This verse holds out a very precious promise, a promise which I desire to apprehend. "....shall see the Lord." We can use scriptural gymnastics to make it appear to say what we want, but, we must be careful. Are we talking about heaven? If so, God says, there are conditions, "...follow peace with all men, and holiness..." This of course creates a dilemma. Is heaven gained by our good works?... emphatically, no! Salvation is through the merits of Jesus Christ, alone. Then are we talking about positional holiness? ie, I'm holy "in Christ"? Well, then it would stand to reason, we would have to be positionally, at "peace with all men", which is not possible. God is saying, there must be a resolve in our hearts to live these out. God does a sovereign work in our hearts, "A new heart also will I give you, and a new Spirit will I put within you:" (see Ezekiel 36:26) that is, God changes us, and in so doing we receive the planting of a deep-seated desire to peruse holiness. It is one of the fruits of salvation. "Knowing it is God which worketh in you both to will and to do of His good pleasure."(Philippians 3:13) Not just for heaven, but for a revelation of the Lord, "...as seeing Him who is invisible." (Hebrew 11:27) Without the reality of Jesus, all we have is His teachings and we need more. We need Christ and His word. That is why revival is imperative, revival brings us to the place where faith is put into action: living out peace with all men and holiness. The result: a Saviour more real than anything we physically see.

Dear reader, is your life holy? If your life is unholy, your heart is unchanged and you are not saved. (Spurgeon) "He shall save His people from their sins." (Matthew 1:21) Not in their sins. For someone to seek God for forgiveness implies repentance. They see themselves as unclean and desire cleansing. No one would cry, "cleanse me" while still in the wallowing hole, no, they would want to first get out and then be clean. Would it not seem ridiculous for God to forgive someone while they continue in their sins. If it looks like a duck, it acts like a duck, and it quacks like a duck, it's a duck. Now, you could call yourself a Christian but if you look like a worldling, act like a worldling and talk like a worldling, then, marvel not that I say unto you, ye must be born again! Now, it is true, you could look like a Christian, act like a Christian, and talk like Christian but unless there has been the peerless work of regeneration in you, make no mistake, you are still in your sins, ye must born again. "Let everyone that nameth the name of Christ depart from iniquity." (2 Timothy 2:19)

One of the reasons we are not seeing revival in this generation is because of our current love affair with this present world. Revival spells holiness, holiness spells, displeasing the world rather than displeasing God. Many of us are just not prepared for the separation. What will people think?... they might mock and chide, "FANATIC!" But, Holiness is like gold, frankincense and myrrh to our blessed Saviour. Will we deprive Him?

Spurgeon writes, "It will be an ill day for the church and the world when the proposed amalgamation shall be complete, and the sons of God and the daughters of men shall be one: then shall another deluge of wrath be ushered in. Beloved reader, be it your aim in heart, in word, in action, in dress to maintain the broad wall, remembering that the friendship of this world is enmity against God." (Jame 4:4)

It was said of the disciples of Jesus that "...they took knowledge of them, that they had been with Jesus." (Acts 4:13). Holiness is to convey a strong family likeness to Jesus. To bear the fruit of Christ, is to have the essence of Christ in you. An apple has in it the essence of the tree. I tell you, we must be so secured, so strong and so deep in Christ, just like a branch to the trunk, until Jesus is all that is visible.

Holiness is, bearing a strong family likeness to Jesus Christ. This happens as the Holy Spirit works in us, what Jesus did for us at the cross. (Chambers) Revival, always reveals two types of deformities, the ones we are unaware of and the ones we try to hide. Holiness is God taking control of our life, "nevertheless I live, yet not I but Christ liveth in me." (Galatians 2:20)

I believe with all my heart that Jesus is coming again. This should prompt us to pursue Jesus Christ with all our hearts. He could come tonight, are you ready? However, I know, we have been waiting a long time and many a Christian has been careless. It is true, Jesus may not come for a long time, but until then, there is another truth, "It is appointed unto men once to die, and after this the judgement."(Hebrews 9:27) We will ALL experience death, until Jesus raptures his church, and death comes at God's appointed time, and it comes to young and old, rich and poor, healthy and the sick. God has not guaranteed any of us another heart beat and there are innumerable ways to die. Are we ready to die? Death,.... It's something we will all experience, but something most of us think little of. "Absent from the body, present with the Lord" (2Corinthians 5:8), writes the apostle, but we act like we don't believe it. A great motivation for revival is the irrefutable fact that we will all stand before Jesus Christ, through death or at His coming. How do we want to appear? Someone says, "When He shall appear, we shall be like Him." (1 John 3:2) Ah, what a wonderful truth, but finish the verse. "Every man that hath this hope in him purifieth himself, even as He is pure." (1John 3:3). God has the refining fire, it's up to us to draw near to the brazen altar.

O! For a reverential, holy fear of God. Do we display the same respect for God as the church of our grandparents? It seems to me we have little respect for others, little respect for self, little respect for those in authority, little respect for the church and the word of God and we have deficient respect for God. I have noticed a pattern over the last thirty years. Our doctrines are watered down, our dress is shabby, our Bible versions are casual, and our worship music more worldly. While some may herald these things as great advancements in the church, I will only mention, that, unlike the church of our grandparents we have not had a single bonafide revival since these have been embraced.

Jesus Christ is coming back, my friend, He is coming for a bride, chaste and pure, therefore, let us serve the divorce papers to all that is of the world. (Ravenhill) Now, I know the prince of this world is not compliant but he has no legal right, not if we have been washed in the blood of the lamb. Serve the papers!

We must keep our motives pure. What does the Word say, "As he which hath called you is holy, so be ye holy in all manner of conversation; because it is written, Be ye holy; for I am holy. (1Peter 1:15,16) I don't see this as a suggestion, and if God commands it, He also makes it possible, and that is good enough for me. However, God is never impressed with a holiness that is like the child who says, "I will do my very best, so mommy will give me a treat." God honours holiness that is one of complete devotion. Not compulsion but devotion. O, that we would see He is worthy and that He gives us the supreme privilege of serving Him In true holiness.

The greatest idol among young people is, the idol of popularity! To this god many have sacrificed their virginity, their virtue, their integrity, and their convictions. Of course, this is not only a young person's idol, many adults have also bowed down to it too. The root of this sacrilege is, people pleasing or self pleasing. But, it is never too late to repent and seek the Lord for forgiveness. In times of an outpouring of God's Spirit we will feel dirty, loathsome, and polluted. David said, "Purge me with hyssop, and I shall be clean: wash me, and I shall be whiter than snow." (Psalm 51:7) The antithesis of this idolatry (and a good deterrent) is to be "fools" for Jesus. He is looking to purify unto Himself a peculiar people... (Titus 2:14) That is: Jesus first, Jesus all the time, Jesus everywhere. This is what a revived church looks like. Strait is the gate, and narrow is the way... (Matthew 7:14) The Christian life is not just entering at the strait gate but walking the narrow way. The narrow way is not just narrow widthwise, but height... you must bow and humble yourself. "For thus saith the high and lofty One that inhabiteth eternity, whose name is Holy; I dwell in the high and holy place, with him also that is of a contrite and humble spirit, to revive the spirit of the humble, and to revive the heart of the contrite ones." (Isaiah 57:15) Revival always brings us to a place of surrender, once again. O Lord bend us.

Why did we go to church today,
to hear a sermon preached?
Or to put in some holy time then quickly to the beach.
Did we meet with God, like Mary, at the Saviour's feet?
Or was an hour wasted, and we only warmed a seat?
Did we wait upon the Lord, in rapture behold our King?
Or did we wish for something else,
like what the world can bring?
Did we worship in spirit and in truth
at the throne of grace?
Or did we sing our favourite tunes
and forget to seek God's face?
If John the Baptist preached today,
I know what he would say,
"Make straight your path,
Cleanse your heart, for Jesus may come today!"

- EDH

I know the word "Puritan" is often in Christian circles used in a disparaging way. No surprise, especially since it is spoken this way by those who have swallowed the stupid, humanistic gospel, which has filled the church with false converts. O! If the church would once again embrace and embody scripture as the Puritans did; if we would love, worship and adore God as they did; if we would obey the word and the Spirit of God as they obeyed; if we would endure hardship and persecution as they did. Then we would give evidence to a real, legitimate revival.

I want to be as holy as God can make a human being, which means, I must be as far from worldliness as is possible. The two cannot mix.

Oh, Lord, most merciful, most kind,
Work your will, in my unholy mind.
Take my heart, my hopes, my dreams,
Consecrate them, to thy loving stream.
Take the water of Thy word; soften this hard clay,
That it be mouldable, upon the Potter's tray.
And when the treadle stops, according to Thy plan,
To thine image may I be, fashioned by Thy hand.
May all I am, all I was, and all I hope to be,
Belong to Jesus only, that He is all men see.

- EDH

Persecution

But he is unworthy of the name of a minister of the gospel of peace who is unwilling not only to have his name cast out as evil but also to die for the truth of the Lord Jesus. It is the character of hirelings and false prophets, who care not for the sheep, to have all men speak well of them. Blessed are you (says our Lord to his first Apostles and in them all succeeding ministers) when men speak all manner of evil against you falsely for my name's sake.

- George Whitefield

....

The early church was married to poverty, prisons and persecutions. Today, the church is married to prosperity, personality, and popularity.

- Leonard Ravenhill

....

There are times when God determines to bring revival and often times this is accomplished through persecution. The cost for following Christ becomes very high. Those who truly are alive to Jesus will gladly follow Him wherever He leads, even through hardship, or through pain, and even if it means loss of property, position or life. And those who are in the body but not of the body; those who have never counted the cost, will turn up their heels against Jesus; they will go back and walk no more with Him. God sovereignly purges, that the church may bring forth more fruit for His glory. It may be persecution is right around the corner. Islam, in foreign lands has flexed its cruel arm and has inflicted many a brother and sister with hideous ill-treatment, imprisonment and murder. While here at home, there are leftist with impassioned zeal who would like nothing better than to deem Christianity and the Bible as toxic, hateful, and as a loathsome bug that needs to be stamped out. Now, there have always been unbalanced people, but dear friend, when the eccentrics of this world are seen as normal and accepted we will have persecution, and Lord willing, revival.

Billy Sunday, the great American evangelist of the late eighteen hundreds stated this, "There are a lot of people in church, doubtless, who have denied themselves—self-denial, for comfort and convenience. There are a lot of people here who never make any sacrifices for Jesus Christ. They will not suffer any reproaches for Jesus Christ. Paul says, 'I love to suffer reproaches for Christ' (Romans 8:17) The Bible says, 'Woe unto you when all men shall speak well of you'. (Luke 6:26). 'Blessed are you when your enemies persecute you.' (Matthew 5:11) That is one trouble in the [North American] church of God today. They are not willing to suffer reproach for God's sake. It would be a godsend if the church would suffer persecution today; she hasn't suffered it for hundreds of years. She is growing rich and lagging behind. Going back."

Shall the head wear the platted thorns while the body rests in carnal ease? (Spurgeon) What says the scriptures? "Yea, and all that will live godly in Christ Jesus shall suffer persecution." (2 Timothy 3:12) Is the church experiencing persecution? Are we personally, as Christians, experiencing persecution? Well, if we are bound, bent and determined to be "Chameleon Christians", meaning: to blend in with the church on Sundays and blend in with the world through the week... we will not. The key phrase in the text is, "Live godly in Christ Jesus." Which means, to walk closely with God. Amos asks, "Can two walk together, except they agree?" (Amos 3:3) To live godly is to have God's presence with us, and to have God's presence, we must be perfectly in agreement with Him. Examine your heart, we must purge every false way. Then is the world crucified unto us and we to the world. (Galatians 6:14)

"Blessed are ye, when men shall revile you, and persecute you, and say all manner of evil against you falsely, for My name's sake." (Matthew 5:11) Persecution comes in many forms. I can say, as a badge of honour, that I have been "reviled for Christ's sake", I have been heckled numerous times, I have had stink bombs tossed at me, I have had a great many disrupters hurl satanic slurs, I have been accosted, I have had nasty messages sent to me through mail and the phone, I have been chased out of a church, I have been maligned, mocked, ridiculed, and this has always left me feeling blessed. The bothersome part, but not surprising, is the way "all manner of evil has been spoken against me." and this from church members. The gospel is offensive and the lukewarm church despises the straightforward gospel. I cannot tell you the unkind things that have been said against me, some out loud and to my face, and others behind my back. Many years ago I began to keep a list of all the hurtful slurs that were hurled at me (it was quite a list too) but, I abandoned it: I felt it was prideful. I think the worst part, in general, is how the church has seen me as an embarrassment. Many have heard how God has used our ministry for revival and to bring souls to Himself, but they would not like to have us come to their churches. Even to acknowledge support for our ministry indicts you by association. I cannot tell you how many times we have preached the truth and souls have trusted in Jesus, but because someone was offended we were never invited back. This is not a pity party, it is a sad reality and the remedy is revival.

It is to be expected by Christians, who are living wholehearted lives for Christ to have their enemies. Jesus said, "The servant is not greater than his Lord, If they have persecuted me, they will also persecute you; if they have kept my sayings, they will keep yours also." (John 15:20). It was said of John Wesley, when he went three days without having anything thrown at him, that he was concerned he must be compromising. Are we concerned?... have we been compromising? However, if we have been shown contempt simply because we have behaved improperly, we deserve it, we have shown ourselves to be hypocrites and we have lost the grand privilege of being Jesus' hands and feet and voice to that soul whom Jesus loves. Even if we insist we are within our rights, die to them. Revival is the experience that revolutionizes the church: evangelism is the expression of the church that reaches the world.

Grant me to stand with my dying Saviour, to be content to be rejected, to be willing to take up unpopular truths, and hold fast despised teachings until death.

-Puritan Prayer, (Valley of Vision)

In evil long I took delight,
Unawed by shame or fear,
Till a new object struck my sight,
And stopped my wild career.

I saw One hanging on a tree,
In agonies and blood;
He fixed His languid eyes on me,
As near His cross I stood.

Sure never till my latest breath,
Shall I forget that look!
It seemed to charge me with His death,
Though not a word He spoke.

A second look He gave, which said,
"I freely all forgive;
This blood is for thy ransomed paid;
I die that thou mayst live."

Thus while His death my sin displays
In all its blackest hue,
Such is the mystery of grace,
It seals my pardon too!

- John Newton

CHAPTER 11

Warfare

ou must expect very frequent and agonizing conflicts with Satan. Satan has very little trouble with those Christians who are not spiritual, but lukewarm, and slothful, and worldly-minded. And such do not understand what is said about spiritual conflicts. Perhaps they will smile when such things are mentioned. And so the devil lets them alone. They do not disturb him nor he them. But spiritual Christians, he understands very well, are doing him vast injury and therefore, he sets himself against them. Such Christians often have terrible conflicts.

-Charles Finney

Beware! Beware!,...whenever we approach revival in the church there is also a revival of opposition. The primary source of this opposition is the devil, and he uses whatever he can to thwart revival, including Christians. One of his greatest tools is discouragement. Maybe you have already felt the piercing of his poisonous dart, I have many times, but "do not lose heart, for we shall reap if we faint not." (Galatians 6:9)

Revival, is not for the faint hearted! Revival requires battle! There is an enemy afoot who detest revival and sets himself in opposition to it. The great deception the devil asserts, (and far too many have been duped by), is that he and his emissaries are an EQUAL opposing force. This is not true, "Greater is He that is in you, than he that is in the world." (1John. 4:4) "The weapons of our warfare are not carnal, but mighty through God to the pulling down of strong holds." (2 Corinthians 10:4) The devil knows his house of cards will fall if we will believe God at His word. But as long as we cower, we should expect the church to remain in a dead state. God told Joshua, "...I will be with thee: I will not fail thee, nor forsake thee." (Joshua 1:5) then God says, in verse 6, "Be strong and of good courage,..." and again, in verse 7, "Only be thou strong and VERY courageous." WE can battle on because God Almighty will not fail.

Standing on the promises I shall not fall.

Martin Luther declared, "I was born to fight devils and factions. It is my business to remove obstruction, to cut down thorns, to fill up quagmires, and to open and make straight paths. But if I must have some failing let me rather speak the truth with too great severity than once to act the hypocrite and conceal the truth."

There are two reasons for entering the fray. 1. An absolute hatred for the enemy: Satan and sin. 2. And an absolute love for our Commander and Chief: the Lord Jesus. Without these attitudes, we will not last long, but with these intense motives, though the battle rages, though casualties are many,... "a thousand shall fall at thy side ten thousand at thy right hand." (Psalm 91:7) and victory seems distant, we will fight on. The Lord's enemies are our enemies, praise God, "We are more than conquerors through Him that loved us." (Romans 8:37)

Watch your enemy. It's very easy to despise or to be repulsed by the hideous, horned devil in a flaming red suit. But God warns us to resist him even when he approaches us as an angel of light (for this is how he most times will seek after us). He is beautiful, radiant, charming, charismatic and he makes absolute sense to our carnal mind. But you will know him because he is a liar, and the father of it. He will start with minor deviations from scripture; little variances no one seems to notice or cares about, but he is very subtle, and patient, and before we know it, we have opened the door to the most heinous, and outrageous sins. Would anyone ever have thought there would be "Christian" denominations that ordain homosexuals? It starts with the little foxes, or just a little fly in the ointment. We need revival.

I entered the house of someone who had a large dog. The owner said, "Don't worry about the dog, he'll probably lick you to death." I'm sure it was meant to ease any fear I might have of being bitten, but as I thought about it, I thought, what a horrible way to die. O, dear friend, the hounds of Hell are out to destroy the church but not with vicious fangs, no, with a much slower, prolonged, insidious death; one that begins with a slimy, deceitful, tickling tongue. How can something so innocuous be a problem? Compromise, diluting of scripture, indifference, apathy, liberalism, and the spirit of slumber are the subtle ways the enemy would lick to DEATH. "Awake, awake; put on strength". (Isaiah 52:1)

Satan laughs a hellish snort! What is it that the foul fiend of hell delights in? Anything that permits him to kill, steal and to destroy. To Kill—the abortion abomination kills, It kills babies but it also kills possibilities. Yesterday the doctor who would have invented a cure for cancer was aborted. Last week a would-be genius who would have invented an answer for world hunger was murdered. To Steal— Esau sold his birthright for a bowl of stew. Judas sold out the Lord for thirty pieces of silver but how many in a fleeting moment have given away their virtue, their virginity, their veracity and their own soul. This is not a bargain, it is outright theft. To Destroy—O the slimy grin he wears at the destruction of lives. He loves to see young people experiment with alcohol and drugs until they are addicted and then they struggle all their lives to be free only to succumb to its ravages on the body: cancer, cirrhosis of the liver, brain damage, kidney failure and the destruction of any dignity they had. He most loves it when his victims advocate for him, "These are my rights!", "This is my body!" The worst of it is when the church keeps quiet. We don't seem to want to interrupt his little party. COME ON!!

But what infuriates that old serpent? What irritates his insidious mind? What grates upon his degraded nerve? What aggravates that slimy snake in the grass? What exasperates his hideous heart? I'll tell you what—a full scaled, full out, Holy Ghost revival. Because, it is when revival comes, the devil's house of cards begins to topple. But, I'm pretty sure this is one of Hell's best kept secrets.

The imagination can be a great source of learning and it can also be the gateway to the most heinous of sins. May our minds be always sprinkled by the blood and sanctified. But follow me as we peer through the grey smoke of the boardroom of the pit where all the Chiefs and Generals of the host of Hell assemble. The topic on this dark and dismal night is, "How to ruin the church!" We might expect some ruckus, mumbling, and shuffling about, then, if it were possible, we might get a glimpse of one of the generals, who thinks he has a grand idea, stand to his feet as he slams his fist with great force against the ancient boardroom table, and with a thunderous sound shouts, "Let us have another round of persecution even as in those days wherein Antipas was a martyr." (Revelation 2:13) We may hear the hideous sounds of much cheering, belching, and snorting but then a highly decorated Commander raises his hand and stands to his feet. I believe I hear him say, "Brothers, it is true the rolling of good Christian heads, the burning of saintly flesh and the torture of the redeemed brings us the greatest satisfaction, and the foulest of joy, but our topic is, 'How to Ruin the Church'. My brothers, you are aware, we have martyrdom presently in many parts of the earth, (from which I find my fondest entertainment) and historically we have attempted to blight the church with great fear, but it has only proven to have made the strong stronger and the pliable to flee. It has caused the faithful to fortify their resolve and has made the hypocrite to leave because of the high cost. Thus, rather than entrench our presence we have weakened our influence and have made the church more courageous and determined. I see four better ways: Liberalism, Materialism, Modernism and dead Fundamentalism."

Liberalism: another Jesus and another gospel, basically, anything goes except the supreme authority of scripture. To say liberalism is an unlikely or an ineffective weapon in the arsenal of Satan would mean, we would have to ignore its casualties: the Presbyterian church, the Anglican or Episcopalian church, the Lutheran church and the Methodist church. Churches at one time synonymous with strong preaching, big faith and great power; how they stood as mighty fortresses for God. Men of renown came forth out of her: Knox, M'Cheyne, Luther, Wesley, and Whitfield. There are, I'm sure, still, some bright shinning lights but I see mostly buzzards hovering over her steeples. Most of these churches are like the Alamo of today: defeated and vacant with the exception of a few actors walking around in costume. Ichabod is written over her gates: the glory of the Lord has departed. Not only has the Lord left but so has the enemy. This I write with a sorrowful and broken heart. But I hear the echo from ancient times, "Can these dry bones live? O Lord God, thou knowest." (Ezekiel 37:3) Please send REVIVAL. But beware, dear reader, this enemy still lurks about and has many a person, many a church, and many a denomination in its sight.

Materialism: an insidious hostile fortification, one that attempts to deify man and "de-deify" God. It is the fixation on the gift rather than the adoration of the gift giver. It is the sin found in John 6:15, "When Jesus therefore perceived that they would come and take him by force, to make Him king,..." and Jesus said v26 ".... Ye seek me, because ye did eat of the loaves, and were filled". It is the, get, gather, gain and keep church, as Ravenhill writes, "Gold is their God and greed is their creed." This gospel is designed to please the flesh. (See John 6:63) Revival always places God in His rightful place, in our hearts, in the church, and in the community.

Modernism: not in the classical sense ie, music, art and literature but by definition a departing or a deviating from generally held practises and the embracing of that which is trending. It has its roots, not in a new Pentecost, but in filling the seats at-any-cost. In many instances, it is to look like the world, to talk like the world and to act like the world. The goal of the enemy here is to water down the truth, or in many cases to avoid fundamental truths that bring conviction: no preaching on redemption through the blood, nor repentance, nor the wrath of God, nor imputed righteousness, nor Hell, nor you must be born again. When the church was birthed, Peter preached, and "they were pricked in their heart". The Trendy church would rather tickle the ear, improve our marriages, fix our bank accounts, and make us feel good about ourselves. However, at Pentecost three thousand souls were saved, they were not just filling seats. "For the time will come when they will not endure sound doctrine; but after their own lusts shall they heap to themselves teachers, (teaching team) having itching ears; and they shall turn away their ears from truth and shall turn unto fables." (2 Timothy 4:3,4) The time is now. By the way, their answer to revival is, "It's not needed." "Thou hast a name that thou livest, and art dead." (Revelation 3:1)

Dead Fundamentalism: dead preachers, preaching dead sermons to dead congregations. Perhaps the grandfather of the most wicked of the enemy's infiltrations. There are precious truths being taught but they are presented as a dead letter; no unction whatsoever. This church dots their "i"s and crosses their "t"s but has heedlessly frostbitten the sheep and scattered the flock, especially youth. This frozen church is the just the right environment for the chilly chosen, their names are, Pharisee, Formalist and Hypocrite. There is nothing wrong with fundamentalism in the literal sense of the word i.e., believing and doing all that the Bible commands. It's the word, "dead" that is the problem. Another word that could apply is, "empty". Empty of any zeal for God or any real inward evidence of the Spirit of God. She is so cold, there is hardly even a heart beat. This church needs the heat of revival for their survival.

This was written with the unmatched skill of the pen of Spurgeon, " It is to be feared that many believers lose their strength as Samson lost his locks, while sleeping on the lap of carnal security". Truer words have never been written. However, I believe it is also true, the revived church, like the revived Samson, is poised to do more violence to our Philistines than that of our former times. A revived church means disaster to the enemy.

A Mighty Fortress is Our God

....

And though this world, with devils filled,
Should threaten to undo us,
We will not fear, for God has willed
His truth to triumph through us:
The Prince of Darkness grim,
We tremble not for him;
His rage we can endure,
For lo! His doom is sure,
One little word shall fell him.

- Martin Luther

Come on soldiers of the cross, may we take your stand boldly, with our banner raised and armour on, against powers, principality and spiritual wickedness in high places and tear down strongholds. If we had spiritual eyes I believe we would see the enemy entrenched in every Bible believing, gospel preaching church; I believe the enemy is most busy when there are revival meetings and evangelistic outreaches. In most cases I believe the foul fiend has worked especially hard to thwart them before they even start, which is why we see so few today. But men and women of old knew about such encampment and they tore down strongholds. What is our problem? Do we not believe there is no weapon formed against us that will prosper?(Isaiah 54:17) John Bunyan poignantly illustrates for us, "When Great-heart came upon Valiant-for-truth, who had just battled against three villainous opponents. He said to Mr Valiant-for-truth, "Thou hast worthily behaved thyself. Let me see thy Sword." So he shewed it him. When he had taken it in hand, and looked there on a while, he said, "Ha, it is a right Jerusalem Blade."

Valiant-for-truth responds, "It is so. Let a man have one of these blades, with a hand to wield it and skill to use it, and he may venture upon an Angel with it. He need not fear its holding, if he can but tell how to lay on. Its edge will never blunt. It will cut flesh and bone and soul and spirit and all." Onward soldier of the cross. "Through God we shall do valiantly: for He it is that shall tread down the enemies." (Ps. 60:12) If God be for us, who can be against us? (Romans 8:31)

ODE TO THE BACKSLIDER

Behold, its told of Peter, "I know you are weak,
The devil's gonna sift you, like a farmer sifts wheat.
But I want you to know, that I've prayed for you son.
And you'll come back to me when the devil is done."

But Peter said to Jesus, "I can handle it Lord,
There ain't know way he can sever this cord,
There ain't know way he can lead me astray,
And there ain't no way Your name I'll betray."

But he was warming himself by the devil's fire,
Feeding the flesh on the sinful desires,
Sin will take you farther than you want to go,
And you'll be ashamed when the rooster crows.

See, I was standing in clover looking over the fence.
Thinking dandelions make more sense.
I was wading in the waters of a heavenly pool.
But the wallowing hole looked so cool.

Think I'll mosey on over, ain't no big deal,
Just wanted to see how the fire would feel.
I ain't hurt' nobody and who's gonna know,
Then I heard the rooster crow.

Grab hold by faith of that rope,
He'll take you off the slippery slope.

It's the mercy of the Lord!

So, don't go warming yourself by the devil's fire.
Feeding the flesh on the sinful desires.
Sin will take you farther than you want to go,
And you'll be ashamed when the rooster crows.

- EDH

CHAPTER 12

Repentance

I f you think you can live in sin and die in peace and then go to heaven, you are being deceived. If you don't accept Christ when you have a healthy body, what makes you think you will when you are dying? The greatest lie that has been believed by so many is that they will be able to make their peace tomorrow— tomorrow is eternity.

- W.P. Nicholson

By now it would be obvious to us all, that there is a desperate need for revival. The question must then be asked, "What can I Do?" In studying revival the one constant in procuring revival is prayer. But, let our first prayer be the prayer of repentance. "But your iniquities have separated between you and your God, and your sins have hid His face from you, that He will not hear." (Isaiah 59:2) If we are to be vessels through which the Lord will usher in a wave of revival, let us wage war against sin in our own lives, turn our hearts completely to Jesus and then let us pour out our souls in sweet intercession for an outpouring of revival in the church. "Who shall ascend into the hill of the Lord? Or who shall stand in His holy place? He that hath clean hands and a pure heart; who hath not lifted up his soul unto vanity, nor sworn deceitfully". (Psalm 24:3,4)

True revival will always bring a deep revulsion for sin. Once we have experienced the exceeding sinfulness of sin we will want to be separated from it. Sin will be loathsome to us, the very sin we embraced will become as a repulsive stink. This is what David meant in Psalm 51 when he said, "Wash me thoroughly from mine iniquity, and cleanse me from my sin." (v2) or "Purge me with hyssop and I shall be clean: wash me, and I shall be whiter than snow. (v7) and "...blot out all mine iniquities."(v9). and, "Create in me a clean heart, O God. (v10) Praise God, He is willing and able to make us clean, "....the blood of Jesus Christ God's Son cleanseth us from ALL sin." (1John 1:7)

David said, "Then will I teach transgressors Thy ways; and sinners shall be converted unto Thee." (Psalm 51:13). God does not use dazzling angels to herald His truth, He uses redeemed sinners who have caught a glimpse of a yawning hell, ready to swallow them, and a bloody Saviour ready to pardon. Revival is the great revealer of heart realities: repentance is the great gift out of which flows fervent evangelism. Conversions is its resolve. David said, "shall be converted".

One of the greatest evangelistic/revival campaigns that ever took place, was around 786-746 BC, during the reign of Jeroboam. God sent a reluctant prophet of Jehovah named Jonah to warn Nineveh, "Yet forty days, and Nineveh shall be overthrown. So the people of Nineveh believed God, and proclaimed a FAST, and put on sackcloth, from the greatest of them to the least of them." (Jonah 3:3,5) Friends, it is time to fast and pray. If we would have revival, it is time to humble ourselves before God. The people of Nineveh did and God saw their sincerity, their deep repentance, and brokenness of heart. Then God showed up with a spectacular display of His grace and the wicked city of one hundred and twenty thousand people turned to the living God.

O, I love how in times of revival, God swiftly calls prodigals unto Himself, just like the father in the parable. "... but when he was a great way off, his father saw him, had compassion, and ran, and fell on his neck, and kissed him." (Luke 15:20) Backsliders never start out to be backsliders, but look how often Jesus has been wounded in the house of His friends. O, to think of the debauchery, the wickedness, the insolence, the uncleanness that is done by those who would name Jesus Christ as their Lord. There is no pain as bitter as that of the Judas-kiss. Yet, Jesus embraces every penitent who comes in repentance to Him. "I will heal their backsliding, I will love them freely: for mine anger is turned away from him". (Hosea 14:4)

Someone says, "But what about David and his sin?" So many use David as an excuse for sinning with impropriety. But wait just a minute. David was king, the great warrior of the Lord, he was also the man after God's own heart, he was the poet of Israel, and God dealt a severe blow of chastisement to him. One which would have sent most of us packing to go back to the world. Do we sincerely think that our sin should receive less than David's? David knew what it was to grieve the heart of God and to put distance between himself and his gracious Lord. Look at his deep repentance, "Renew a right spirit within me." (Psalm 51:11) David is crying out to God for personal revival: RENEW. There are seven penitential psalms in the Bible: Psalms 6, 32, 38, 51, 102, 130, 143 Read them. David wrote, "I am weary with my groaning; all the night make I my bed to swim; I water my couch with tears." (Psalm 6:6,7) O, we can sin with David but can we repent like him?

Listen to the prophet speak to the miserable sinner, "Let the wicked forsake his way and the unrighteousness man his thought: and let him return unto the Lord, and He will have mercy upon him; and He will abundantly pardon." (Isaiah 55:6) O, grace, grace, marvellous grace, such hope for sinners. Who but God could contrive such a design, that He could be just and justify the guilty. How precious is the blood of Jesus that makes us white as snow. And look,... for the one who returns, God does not just pardon, but abundantly pardons. Look as God sits at the judgment bar of heaven and judges in righteousness. For God to pardon a vile, but penitent sinner is nothing short of a miracle. But for God to put him in right standing through the imputed righteousness of His dear Son is an act of even greater grace. But for the Judge to adopt the criminal into His own family and call him son or daughter is a blessing beyond imagination. Now, to take it one step further, for God to take the sinner to His own palace and makes him heir and joint heir with Jesus, that is to be abundantly pardoned. (Spurgeon) Come prodigals, turn around, away with the hogs, the husks, and the harlots, though you have injured your Friend, your best Friend, yet, He will receive you.

Andrew Murray writes, "Until the sin is known and mourned over, publicly confessed and condemned, and men are ready to be led by the Holy Spirit to a life entirely devoted to God and His service, prayer for revival will not avail."

O, come to the altar. The Father's arms are open wide. Yes, we come to the altar, but we come with no excuses, no pretence, no performance, and with nothing pharisaical. We do not come as a slave to a master trembling, no, we come as a sorrowing child to a benevolent Father: we come with penitent tears because we have wounded Him, and grieved Him. Ah,... but when we come and place our hand upon the head of our redeeming Sacrifice we find cleansing, liberty, remission and reconciliation. Jesus paid it all! But the dignified gospel has taken the place of the rustic church altar. I am surprised at how many good ole gospel songs include in their lyrics, how penitent souls came to an old fashioned altar, when on their knees in prayer they found the Saviour. I have also noticed, the old fashioned altar mentioned in numerous testimonies of the saints; entire families came forward and were saved at evangelistic meetings and revival services . But I hear someone say, "We don't do that any more, we are much too dignified for that." "Jesus also, that He might sanctify the people with His own blood, suffered", (naked), "without the gate." (Hebrews 13:12) Is there any dignity here? Job said at the revelation of almighty God, "I have heard of Thee by the hearing of the ear: but now mine eye seeth Thee. Wherefore I abhor myself, and repent in dust and ashes." (Job 42:4,5) Revival will alway reveal the awesomeness of God and the depravity of man. There is still an altar, for the lost and for the broken.

Some things are useless broken. A broken glass is not fit to drink from, or a broken rail is not safe to lean on. Some things are better broken: Mary's alabaster box of ointment of spikenard was very valuable but useless until it was broken and during revival "a broken and contrite heart God will not despise". (Psalm 51:17) It is only then, that the genuine contents are revealed. God during revival makes us broken bread and poured out wine. Bread becomes bread when the grain is crushed, it is broken. Wine becomes wine when the grapes are crushed. Again, it has to be broken. Do you, my dear reader, know anything about the brokenness of repentance experimentally? Have you been broken? The Psalmist said, "I am like a broken vessel" (Psalm 31:12) "Make me to hear joy and gladness; that the bones which Thou hast broken may rejoice." (Psalm 51:8)

Welsh Revival 1904

Drunkenness was immediately cut in half, and many taverns went bankrupt. Crime was so diminished that judges were presented with white gloves signifying that there were no cases of murder, assault, rape or robbery or the like to consider. The police became unemployed in many districts. Stoppages occurred in the coal mines, not due to unpleasantness between management and workers, but because so many foul-mouthed miners became converted and stopped using foul language that the horses which hauled the coal trucks in the mine could no longer understand what was being said to them.
Welsh revival 1904. -J. Edwin Orr

Belfast Revival 1922-1923

During the Belfast revival at the shipyard of Harland and Wolff a shed named "the Nicholson Shed" was erected to house stolen tools that newly converted workers were returning as a result of Nicholson's preaching.

Work in me more profound and abiding repentance;
Give me the fullness of a godly grief that trembles
and fears,
Yet ever trusts and loves, which is ever powerful,
and ever confident;
Grant that through the tears of repentance
I may see more clearly the brightness and glories of
the saving cross.
-Puritan Prayer, (Valley of Vision)

Sweet altar, precious altar, blessed altar, in most of our churches, deserted altar. The altar is a place of death, but it's also a place of life "...nevertheless I live; yet not I, but Christ liveth in me:.. " (Galatians 2:20). It is also a place of humbleness, a place of confession, a place of contrition and repentance, without which, the altar is a mere hypocritical formality. "I beseech you therefore, brethren, by the mercies of God, that ye present your bodies a living sacrifice, holy, acceptable unto God, which is your reasonable service." (Romans. 12:1) When we die to self we can live to Jesus and not before.

TRUST AND OBEY

But we never can prove
The delights of His Love
Until all on the altar we lay;
For the favour He shows
And the joy He bestows
Are for them who who will trust and obey.

- John H. Sammis. 1887

THE OLD ALTAR

....

I can't understand why some folk will demand
Christ's blood be left out of our creed;
That blood paid the cost of all who are lost,
And it's flow is all that we need.

I think of that night lost and tired of my plight,
I knelt at the bench in the straw;
I parted with sin, the Spirit came in,
The beauties of heaven I saw.

- Cecil Truesdell 1944

O, that I might constantly live a life repenting of sin.

CHAPTER 13

Fear of the Lord

A s God, from the beginning has worked prominently through revivals, there can be no denial of the fact that revivals are part of the divine plan.

-E.M. Bounds

There have always been false prophets, false teachers and false doctrines. The great travesty is when the church begins to embrace insidious error as harmless. This can only happen when there is no longer a reverent fear of the Lord and the Word of God no longer holds supreme authority in our lives. Revival drives the church to uphold truth at any cost and magnifies Jesus on His throne as the King eternal, in whom all majesty is ascribed. Beware of what you agree to and declare through your singing. There are little twists that are noxious to the soul. Watch what you swallow in seemingly innocent little messages. Better to be mocked as a Puritan than to be cheered as pliable.

We live in incredible times, it would seem that we know very well the science of marketing. This science is deep and effective and we have brought it into the church. Why not make church more marketable, why not make it fun, brighter, livelier, why not draw in an audience and hit them with the gospel? Is that what Jesus did? It would appear to me Jesus did not make it easier but more difficult. "Except ye eat the flesh of the Son of Man, and drink his blood, ye have no life in you." (John 6:53) From that time many of the disciples went back and walked no more with Him. (Jn. 6:65) What? Did Jesus miss a terrific marketing opportunity? Jesus said, Unto you is given to know the mysteries of the kingdom of God: but to others in parables; that seeing they might not see, and hearing they might not understand." (Matthew 8:10) The seeker sensitive movement has blighted the church across denominational lines. Ask yourself if what you are seeing now, in your church, would have even been considered fifteen years ago. I'm not saying we shouldn't make improvements, I'm not saying the church does not evolve. But I would only ask that we consider how it is possible the churches in deepest darkest Africa, or China or the Middle East have a stronger church than we do and without the bells and whistles. There was once a missionary from China who travelled to the United States and when he returned everyone was excited to hear what he had found most interesting about the American Church, he replied, "I am amazed at how much they are able to accomplish without God."

The "Trendy Church" runs counter to true revival! We visited a church while on vacation, their motto was, "Family, Fun, Messy, and Laughter". The thought behind this clever chain of words is, "We are the, 'down to earth' church; we have the 'down to earth' pastor, the 'down to earth worship team', and 'down to earth prayers." Someone says, "This is the church I'm looking for!" But wait just a minute, is this the church Jesus is looking for. The Bible says, "He that is of the earth is earthly, and speaketh of the earth:...". (John 3:31). Revival is not earthly but rather, it is heavenly. "If ye then are risen with Christ, seek those things which are above". (Colossians 3:1) I heard a young man give a missions report the other day. He said, "In the apostle Paul's day it was not "COOL" to be a Christian. I have news for him, it has never been "COOL" to be a Christian, yet, the "Trendy Church" is desperately trying to make it appear so. Look, "COOL" is to cold, as lukewarm is to hot, they both make Jesus sick. (See Revelation 3:16). As long as we are satisfied with the earthly we will have no desire for the heavenly. This is why Jesus said, "Behold,

I stand at the door and knock." (Revelation 3:20). How awful, Jesus, is left outside the church!

Revival in the flesh is often tried but always falls short of any true and lasting results; fleshly revival is a contradiction of terms. Revival is spiritual and can only be apprehended by a living, active faith.

The last thing my pastor used to say to me when I went to minister the gospel was, "Preach for a verdict." That is, let everyone be absolutely certain: guilty or not guilty. If judgment must begin at the house of God (1 Peter 4:17) let everyone choose: spirit of the world or the Spirit of God. Self love will always choose the spirit of the world. Elijah's words hold for the church also, "How long halt ye between two opinions? if the Lord be God, follow Him: but if Baal, then follow him." (1Kings 18:21) Revival will always bring us to the place where we will love Jesus more than self, or sin, or the spirit of the world.

In the last little while I have had two pastors tell me they were afraid to preach. I find this encouraging. It is healthy to have a holy fear when approaching the sacred desk. The man who puts preaching on the same level as addressing a sales meeting, or a lecture on finances, or a lesson on, how to disarm a time bomb, is not worthy to preach the gospel. The preaching of the gospel is infinitely more dire. For to some, heaven and hell hang in the balance, and the preacher will have to give an account of his ministry to the Lord. (See Hebrews 13:17, James 3:1) When all the evidence is compiled at the Great White Throne Judgement may there be no one who will be a able point a finger at us and say, we did not warn them.

O for a reverential fear of the Lord. Consider the Pharisee: the thorn in the flesh of Jesus. But what was it about them that disturbed Him most? Was it their strict adherence to the law? or that they were nit pickers? No, I don't think so. It was their hypocrisy, "But all their works they do to be seen of man." (Matthew 23:5). They had an outward exhibition without an inward evidence. Jesus said of them, "Woe unto you, scribes and Pharisees, hypocrites! For you are like whited sepulchres which indeed appear beautiful outward, but are within full of dead men's bones and all uncleanness. (Matthew 23;27) Jesus is looking for the genuine article. I can tell you that His displeasure is not only aimed at the Pharisees but all hypocrites. I know a man who is living with a woman he is not married to. If you ask him, he will say he's a Christian. Jesus calls him a liar (1John 2:4) I know another man who is a practising homosexual and he'd say, he's a born again believer. Jesus calls him a fraud. (1Corinthians. 6:9,10) I know many, so called, Christians who are enamoured with the world, and Jesus derides them as enemies, hypocrites. (James 4:4) And still others, who are leaders in the church, will boldly proclaim, "Have we not prophesied in Thy name? And in Thy name cast out devils? And in Thy name done many wonderful works? And then Jesus professes unto them, I never knew you: depart from me, ye that work iniquity." (Matt. 7:22,23) I think an evangelical hypocrite is worse than the Pharisee; we have the full cannon of scripture, they did not.

"Let us search and try our ways, and turn again to the Lord." (Lam. 3:40) Why do so many falter on the wrong road? Is it because many are guilty of taking the path most travelled? Many travel the destructive broadway; only few travel God's chosen, narrow, way of life. "Turn again", spells, REVIVAL. The road of the Lord is the road of obedience. Jesus said, "I do only those things that please the Father. " (Jn. 8:29) We only have one master to please.

> The dearest idols I have known,
> Whate'er that idol be;
> Help me to tear it from Thy throne'
> And worship only Thee.

> Revive deep spirituality in my heart:
> Let me live near to the great Shepherd,
> hear His voice, know it's tones, follow its calls.
> Keep me from deception by causing me to abide
> in the truth,

from harm by helping me walk in the power
of the Spirit.
Give me intenser faith in the eternal verities,
burning into me by experience the things I know;
Let me never be ashamed of the truth of the gospel,
that I may bear reproach,
vindicate it
see Jesus as its essence,
know in it the power of the Spirit.
Lord, help me, for I am often lukewarm and chilly;
unbelief mars my confidence,
sin makes me forget thee.
Let the weeds that grow in my soul be cut
at their roots;
Grant me to know that I truly live only
when I live to Thee,
that all else is trifling.
Thy presence alone can make me holy, devout,
strong and happy.
Abide in me, gracious God.
- Puritan Prayer (The Valley of Vision)

Someone says, It would seem, there are only a few who care about revival." Not so, God wants revival. Do you think God is happy with a, dull, lethargic, indifferent, petulant, apathetic, materialistic, bickering, pride filled, murmuring church? No way! "Well then" somebody says," since God is for revival, we shall surely have it." Not so, it's not that God needs convincing, but, it would seem, God needs to convince the church. Have we cried out to God? "Yes, Lord, we desire to have revival." Have we expressed our desire by what we are willing to give up? Our time, our leisure, our stupid TVs, our vices, our sin, and our apathy. Notice, I did not say money, ten million dollars will not bring revival, the best bands, the most brilliant light shows, the most gifted preachers, the greatest programs, WILL NOT BRING REVIVAL. Jesus said, "Behold, I stand at the door, and knock...."

Excuses for the absence of revival:

1. We are too distracted and busy with other things.
2. It costs too much: too much time, too much money, too much to give up, too much spiritual exertion, too much physical effort, and too much planing.
3. We can't bring back the past and God doesn't seem to work in the church that way anymore.
4. We are far too sophisticated and dignified for such revivals.
5. No one seems interested.
6. We just don't need it.

The foul fiend of hell couldn't agree more. We do not need excuses we need resolve.

CHAPTER 14

Is Revival Needed?

f our ears are open to God's voice, and our hearts respond fully to His leading, I believe we are on the eve of unusual revivals of religion.

- D.L. Moody, published just before his death

Is revival needed?

There are some who ask this question out of ignorance, some from immaturity and others from stupidity. If this question can be asked at all, it is a clear sign revival is needed. Oh, the devil has tucked some to sleep so comfortably, so soundly, all that can be heard from them is, "Do not disturb!"

I tell you, when the world influences the church rather than the church influencing the world, it is a sure indication we are in need of revival. When we no longer battle against the world, the flesh and the devil it is clear we need revival. Do not tell me, "it does not matter: our church is just adapting to the culture." No, let's call it what it is, compromise! "Ye adulterers and adulteresses, know ye not that friendship with the world is enmity with God? whosoever therefore will be a friend of the world is the enemy of God." (James 4:4)

When the world treats the church like a dog, it is time for

revival! When the world tethers a leash around her neck and drags her into its ideology, when the world puts up an electric fence and says, "Hitherto thou shalt go but no further."(Job 38:11), when the world fastens a bark collar around her throat and warns her "to stifle your voice", it is high time for revival! "And the very gates of hell shall not prevail against her." (See Matthew 16:18)

Unbridled lust best describes our present world. Now, the world has always lived on the edge of the abyss of lust, but now it has jumped in with both feet and there seems to be no bottom. No amount of real factual science can abate the alarming downhill assent. Our world has lost its moral compass and the church has also been dragged along by degrees. On the other hand, when revival comes the reverse is true, the church once again becomes salt and light and pulls the world back. Our answer to the cruel act of abortion is revival. Our best argument against the insidious, repulsive, homosexual agenda is revival. Our defence against the greed-driven marijuana industry is REVIVAL. History has shown when revival comes, the filth of the world also feels the heat from the Refiner's fire.

I'm looking forward to the kind of revival that will increase the rate of unemployment. I'm looking forward to seeing bartenders out of work because pubs and bars do not have enough patrons. I want to see the fortune telling businesses closed down, the pimps nonexistent, drug dealers dispersed. I'm anticipating a time when police officers are laid off, because there is not enough crime and prisons have to close down. I can't wait to see casinos vacant and become a habitation of bats, lizards and other vermin. The devil and his emissaries cannot stand in the midst of a full scaled, Holy Ghost revival. O, that we might see it! O! That we might see it!

But Someone says, "Can we not leave things as they are and do without revival?" Yes,... yes we can, but then we will have bought into the greatest of all deceptions, the lie that, the status quo is good enough. We have been so long without revival that we have accepted the idea that living below God's prescribed spiritual level is ok. Have we not become weak, and cold, and sickly, and sleepy and dry and dead and inert. Well, I for one am sick of it. I am praying for revival until we get it.

What is a coasting Christian? A coasting Christian is one who coasts through their Christian life, just religious enough to fit in well with the church community. Church every now and then, a little offering here and there, generally moral and upright, but, not too religious, that he doesn't fit in with the world. This type of person represents the largest people group in the church. A coasting business man sees little profit, a coasting employee sees no advancement and a coasting soldier is an easy target for the enemy. May the Lord deliver us from such an odious spirit.

I see five Christian types as we approach revival:

1. The ignorant: "What is revival?"
2. The indolent: "I've no time for revival"
3. The insolent: "There is no revival anymore"
4. The reluctant: "I hope God brings revival."
5. The militant: " There is revival coming."

We will know them by their prayers. Let's listen in.

1. The ignorant: "What is revival? (Well, nothing here)
2. The indolent: "O, Lord send someone to bring revival."
3. The insolent: Silence (They don't think revival is needed, They say in their hearts, "You can have your little revival but don't expect anything from me. Revival's not worth it, too much trouble for a whole lot of enthusiasm.")
4. The reluctant: O God,... If thou canst do anything, bring revival. (They want revival, but they do not really expect to see it.")
5. The militant: He/she storms heaven's citadel with strong, fervent, unceasing prayers and tears. "Lord give us revival lest we die!"

But someone says, "HOPELESS,...Revival is hopeless!" I will go one step farther. It is impossible,... But, God works in the realm of the impossible. If it were possible we wouldn't need God. For Sarah to bear Isaac, impossible; for Moses to part the Red Sea, impossible; for little David to slay Goliath, impossible; for God to take on human flesh and dwell amongst us, impossible. "For with God nothing shall be impossible." (Luke 1:37) "Wherefore he saith, Awake thou that sleepest, and arise from the dead, and Christ shall give thee light." (Ephesians 5:14)

We tend to look at our spiritual problems from the symptoms, God looks to the source. We see the effect, He sees the cause. To us the fruit is most important but to God it is the root. If we would look to the root, we would see we need revival. The devil would like to keep us distracted, "Keep your eyes on the symptoms but whatever we do, do not have revival." Why?... Because when real revival ignites, it is a fire that is too difficult for him to put out. WE can grieve the Spirit, WE can quench the Spirit, but try as he may, and he will try, he will not succeed. It is better for him if revival never starts.

During the pastor's morning message he boldly declared, "We need revival in Canada!" Then he followed up by asking, "How many would like to see revival in our land?" Two people shouted, "Amen" my wife and I. Now there were, mind you, over two hundred and fifty people in the church. He then leaned forward and cupped his hand to his ear and with a louder, more emphatic tone, he asked again, "How many would like to see revival in our land?" Another dozen or so chimed in, "Amen" Then my pastor spoke these dolorous words, "Some people do not want to see revival in Canada." This is still ringing in my head. I'm not sure, can you even call yourself a Christian if you do not want revival? This, to me, is a sad reality, of an obvious truth, that we need revival.

I accept the fact that revival is according to God's good pleasure. He brings revival where He will and He denies revival where He will. I have been praying for revival and I have been preaching revival for many years and I will continue to do so. Someone says, "Perhaps God is not going to bring revival." Maybe so, but I have never heard Him tell me so, therefore until He does, revival it is.

Does anyone know what people were saying just prior to the Welsh revival of 1904? Most likely the naysayers were saying, "God doesn't work through revivals anymore!" Or how about what folks were saying just before the Hebrides revival? Maybe, "Things have gotten too bad, not even God could revive our dead churches". And what were the doubters chattering about on the cusp of The Great Awakening? In all probability they were saying, "This is not like the old days, why it's 1730, we are too dignified and we have too many distractions to have any meaningful revival. Besides, church attendance is good and offerings are quite sufficient, there's no need for revival here." Does any of these sound familiar?

Who needs revival?
This is a test.
Now, be brutally honest with yourself.
Do you have a burden for lost souls?
Do you have a desire for personal holiness?
Do you have a hunger for God's word? (Comfort)
Do you have longing for sweet intimacy with Jesus?

If you have answered no to these questions, well, let me put it this way. If you were a patient in a cardiac ward, the doctor would declare, "There are little to no vital signs, get the defibrillator this patient needs to be revived."

Many years ago, when my wife Cathy was driving school bus, it became obvious there was a problem with the bus when her stop arm would barely open. She called the mechanic and explained the problem and they rushed out to fix it. The problem was, the battery had grown weak. When the new battery was installed the sign whipped out in an instant. It was then she realized, there had been a problem for a long time, but because it happened in a very slow incremental way it wasn't noticeable. Our spiritual walk can sometimes be like that, slowly and subtly we grow weaker, colder, more apathetic and compromising, just like the frog in boiling water. Revival is like getting a new battery.

I hear someone say, "Oh, wretched man that I am, I can not lay hold of revival. Sin clings to me like fly paper and the devil is like a hound, always at my heels." Poor soul, I, also, have been in your shoes. Here is what I have found. Head for the cross!... The devil hates the cross. He hates the blood because it reminds him of his ultimate defeat. "For the preaching of the cross is to them that perish foolishness; but unto us which are saved it is the power of God." (1 Corinthians 1:18)

> Oh, the bitter shame and sorrow
> That a time could ever be
> When I let the Saviour's pity
> Plead in vain, and proudly answered:
> All of self and none of Thee!
>
> Yet He found me; I beheld Him
> Bleeding on th' accursed tree,
> Heard Him pray: "Forgive them, Father!;
> And my wistful heart said faintly:
> Some of self and some of Thee!"
>
> Day by day His tender mercy,
> Healing, helping, full and free,
> Sweet and strong and, ah! so patient,
> Brought me lower, while I whispered:
> Less of self and more of Thee!
>
> Higher than the highest heaven,
> Deeper than the deepest sea,
> Lord, Thy love at last has conquered;
> Grant me now my spirit's longing
> None of self and all of Thee!

- Theo Monod (1875)

CHAPTER 15

The Cross

If you have not yet found out that Christ crucified is the foundation of the whole volume, you have hitherto read your Bibles in vain. Your religion is a heaven without a sun, an arch without a key-stone, a compass without a needle, a clock without a spring or weights, a lamp without oil. It will not comfort you. It will not deliver your soul from hell.

-J.C. Ryle

The one great rival to revival is the spirit of the world. The reason we see so little or no revival in the church today is because we are too enamoured by the world. The remedy to this, is the cross of Jesus Christ. The more we contemplate on the sufferings of our dear Redeemer dealt to Him by the world, the less love we will hold to it. The world's smiles will not attract anymore and its frowns will bring no fear. The world will become vile to us and we will be of no use to the world. The apostle Paul wrote, "But God forbid that I should glory, save in the cross of our Lord Jesus Christ, by whom the world is crucified to me, and I to the world." (Galatians 6:14) Paul never lost sight of the cross and lived his entire Christian life in a perpetual state of revival.

Revival must always bring us back to the ground of the reality of redemption. I remember my pastor frequently saying, "We do not worship the 'wood' of the cross, that would be idolatry, but we worship the Saviour for the 'work' of the cross." I read this poignant piece form the Valley of Vision, Puritan Prayer, "The blood that was shed on Calvary's cross was that of incarnate God, its worth is infinite, its value beyond measure. Infinite must be the evil and the guilt that requires so high a payment." The reality of the redemption ignites our heart to burn with a sincere love for Jesus.

O the deep, deep love of Jesus; He, "Who loved me and gave Himself for me." (Galatians 2:20) There, there on Calvary's Hill, behold, the crucified Jesus. Look, as every drop of blood that gushes from His wounds—His hands, His feet, His brow, His ploughed back all say, "I love you!" Every salty tear that stands in His eyes and descends down His bruised cheeks and plucked beard, cries, "I love you!" Every groan, every sigh, every breath, declares "I love you!". Every pearl of briny sweat distilled from His feverish flesh as it runs down His naked body and plummets to the earth, shouts, "I love you!" Every moment of mental anguish repeats, "I love you!" What more could He do? It is this kind of love that will make men to be repulsed by their idols, to have a loathing for the world and will make them to stop loving self.

There is only one ground on which a Holy God and sinful man can meet, and that is at the cross of Jesus Christ. If we bypass the cross we have no hope for reconciliation with God. A lake of blood from sacrificed animals, a mountain of ashes from burnt offerings, rivers of remorseful tears, a list a mile long of good works could never remove one sin, but, hallelujah, the blood of Jesus Christ God's Son cleanseth us from ALL sin. (1John 1:7) My one defence is NOT MY righteousness. Whenever we include the words "my" and "righteousness" we are speaking only of filthy rags in God's sight. (Isaiah 64:6) No, "my hope is built on nothing less than Jesus blood and righteousness." Do you know why many of our church services are dead?.... active yes, with noise, and movement yes, but dead? The true worshipper knows this,—Because they are bloodless. The life, my dear reader, is still in the blood. (See Leviticus 17:11) And never was there a revival brought about in the church but by preaching the doctrine of the imputed righteousness of Christ through the blood.

This, as the man of God, Martin Luther calls it, "articulus stantis aut cadentis ecclesiae", "The article by which the church stands or falls."

O the wonderful cross of Jesus Christ!... but, what part does it play in revival? Revival is not some holy buzz. Revival in its entirety is based solely on the redemption. At the cross we can get a fresh glimpse of our Saviour's sacrifice, by which we receive abundant pardon, imputed righteousness, peace with God, adoption as sons, rescue from hell's grasp, new birth, reception of the Holy Ghost, eternal life and much more. There is something else we must see. Without the cross there could be no resurrection. There is no topic the apostles preached on more in the New Testament than the resurrection. Why? Because, the cross is the gateway by which we now are permitted to enter into the resurrected life. The very word resurrection implies revival. Many have come to the cross but in this generation few have gone beyond. It is the resurrection life which enables us to live out what the cross did for us. Paul wrote to the Philippians, "That I may know Him, and the power of His resurrection..." (Philippians 3:10)

The death, burial, and resurrection of Jesus Christ is unfathomably deep. Most of the time we resemble the swallows. We are content to just skim the surface. But revival plunges us into the deep, where we can get a deeper appreciation for His sacrifice. In times of revival God increases our capacity to consume more of God, richer morsels of God, and sweeter blessings from God. This is what the Bible calls, the fullness of God. What would happen if an entire church experienced such a move of God. He has done it before, why not do it for us and for our church?

Listen as the preacher utters this sentence, "If you were the only sinner on earth Jesus would have come and died for you." Do you believe that? Well, I believe it. But if you were the only sinner, who would have nailed Him to the cross? It could not have been the Jews, not the Roman soldiers, not the religious elite. Jesus could have nailed His own feet and maybe one hand but it would have been impossible to complete the task. Who would have cried, "Crucify Him"? Who would have plucked His beard and spit in His face? Who would have mocked Him? Who would have lacerated his body with the whip? Who would have plaited a crown of thorns and jammed it into His skull? Who would have lifted the Son of Man and plunged His cross into the earth? Who would have raised the sponge of vinegar to His parched lips? Who? Who? Who? If you were the only sinner, it would have had to be you. You see, I assert that it was you, it was your sin and my sin. But listen close, listen as Jesus breathes these sweet words to the penitent sinner, "Father forgive them…" (Luke 23:34) and the Father always answers the Son's prayers.

We will never understand the cross until we gaze into the word "substitute". Have you ever come to the cross and laid your hand on the head of Jesus and confessed your sin? Have you ever transferred your guilt to the perfect, spotless Lamb of God?.....Every lie, every foul word, every lustful thought, every wicked imagination, every blasphemous utterance and act, every sexual sin, every idol erected, every disobedience, every rebellious act, every hateful, murderous, venomous desire, every theft, every covetous dream, all these, and ten thousand more? This is not nebulous, it must be clear, concentrated and deliberate. Our sin is to be transferred to the Innocent. That is mercy. What we receive in its place is the imputed righteousness of Jesus. That is grace. "God hath made Him to be sin for us, who knew no sin; that we might be made the righteousness of God in Him." (2Corinthians 5:2). H. Spafford wrote, "My sin, oh, the bliss of this glorious thought, my sin, not in part but the whole, is nailed to the cross, and I bear it no more, praise the Lord, praise the Lord O my soul." I beg you to do this now, right now.

"O, Thanks be unto God for His unspeakable gift." (1Corinthians 9:15) Jesus Christ is the gift unto this world, for which we all can find reason to be thankful. Even the lost. My dear friends, even you who are estranged from the covenant of grace; lost and dead in sins, even you must give thanks to God for Jesus. All the reasons would take up too much space and time but you must realize that it is by His infinite mercy you are not consumed. You must see that God is disgusted with you. You are a rebel to Him, an anarchist in your heart…. He has heard your thoughts say, "We will not have this man to rule over us." (Luke 19:14) God is ready, and is within His right, to damn you to hell for all eternity. But for the moment His hand is stayed. Instead, He stretches out His loving arms and bids you to come to Him with childlike faith, by trusting in the all sufficient merits of His dear Son, alone. As the hymn writer says in one of our carols, "Peace on earth, and mercy mild, God and sinners reconciled" Oh, if I thought I could convince you to turn to Jesus by my clever arguments, I would write all day long until my fingers would cramp up and then I would use my toes or any other means, to tell you to come. Trust Him.

WHEN I SURVEY

When I survey the wondrous cross
On which the Prince of glory died,
My richest gain I count but loss
And pour contempt on all my pride.

Forbid it, Lord, that I should boast
Save in the death of Christ my God.
All the vain things that charm me most
I sacrifice them to His blood.

See from His head, His hands, His feet
Sorrow and love flow mingled down.
Did e'er such love and sorrow meet
Or thorns compose so rich a crown?

Were the whole realm of nature mine
That were an offering far too small.
Love so amazing, so divine
Demands my soul, my life, my all.

- Issac Watts 1707

Christ was all anguish that I might be all joy,
Cast off that I might be brought in,
Trodden down as an enemy
That I might be welcomed as a friend,
Surrendered to hell's worst
That I might attain heaven's best,
Stripped that I might be clothed,
Wounded that I might be healed,
Athirst that I might drink,
Tormented that I might be comforted,
Made a shame that I might inherit glory,
Entered darkness that I might have eternal light.
My Saviour wept that all tears
might be wiped from my eyes,
Groaned that I might have endless song,
Endured all pain that I might have unfading health,
Bore a thorny crown that I might have a
glory-diadem,
Bowed his head that I might lift up mine,
Experienced reproach that I might receive welcome
Closed His eye in death
that I might gaze on unclouded brightness,
Expired that I might forever live.
O Father, who spared not thine only Son that Thou
mightest spare me,
All this transfer thy love designed and accomplished;
Help me to adore Thee by lip and life.
- A Puritan Prayer "Love Lustres At Calvary"
(Valley of Vision)

This is Love

Can you comprehend love, define its boundaries?
Can you measure it in miles,
or is it measured by degrees?
Can you lay it out, and mark it down;
does love have a size?
No you cannot see love, till you've seen the crucified!

My friend, are you still searching?
Is there sill an empty space?
You've searched high and low,
and in every barren place.
Are you looking for the kind of love
that fills soul's poverty?
Look upon the hill, I see love at Calvary!

Chorus

This is love, by His hand He showed the breadth.
At Calvary His life was poured out unto death.
This is love, by His hand He showed the length.
By God's mighty power in weakness is our strength.
This is love, by His feet He showed the depth.
O' how far He plunged to save a sinful wretch.
This is love, by the thorns He showed the height.
Behold the Lamb that's slain to purchase us new life.
This is love, the cross is love, the cross, the cross is love.

- EDH

CHAPTER 16

Hell

*G*od's time for revival is the very darkest hour, when everything seems hopeless. It is always the Lord's way to go to the very worst cases to manifest His glory.

- Andrew Murray

The telling of the creation story and the enlightening of Bible prophecies are great teachings God uses to awaken sinners, which is essential. (see chapter 1) Its primary use is not salvation, although it is possible someone might come to faith in Jesus through them. Hell is also used in the same way, to awaken sinners. It's not primarily used for salvation. Many will hear the message of hell or the wrath of God and fear will drive them to Christianity for refuge. But typically this response merely stems from self love, they do not want to burn. This does not mean we forget about this powerful doctrine, as many preachers have, but rather we need to preach it boldly, and with tears. Spurgeon wrote, "Never let us speak of the doom of the wicked harshly, flippantly, or without holy grief. For the loss of heaven and the endurance of hell, must always be themes for tears. For to live without Christ is grief enough, but to die without Him is an overwhelming horror, that should grind our hearts to powder as we fall on our faces and cry, 'Oh God, have mercy upon them, for Thy grace and love's sake.'"

The abandoned doctrine of Hell. I hate the preaching of Hell, but I will and must trample my feelings, my preferences, and my desires under foot, for the sake of the lost. Not that Hellfire and brimstone saves anyone, if it would, I would never stop preaching it. If someone only comes to Jesus to escape wrath, their interest is merely self love. But when we see Jesus crucified, when we see the length He went, the depth He plunged to save us from the due punishment for our sin, we shall behold Him with love unfeigned. When we get a glimpse of the burnings, the torments, the anguish of Hell we will cry out to the living God in grateful chorus and then plead for precious souls, especially those of our own house. There will be an urgency in our evangelism, "...knowing therefore the terror of the Lord, we persuade men." (2 Corinthians 5:11) "And of some have compassion, making a difference: and others save with fear pulling them from the fire; hating even the garment spotted by the flesh." (Jude 22, 23). Yet this preaching will bar me from a great many churches, evangelical churches.

John the Baptist had no problem boldly proclaiming his message to the masses, and it was not, run to the grace of God, but "Flee the wrath to come." The Angel of the Lord, cried out, "Escape for thy life, look not behind thee, neither stay thou in the plain; escape to the mountains lest thou be consumed." (Genesis19:17) The Bible says of Noah, he was moved with love, no, "By faith Noah, being warned of God of things not seen as yet, moved with FEAR, prepared an ark to the saving of his house;..." (Hebrews 11:7)

Jonathan Edwards preached that awful message at Enfield Connecticut in 1741 that sparked the great awakening. What was its title? "Sinners in Hand of an Angry God!" O, for another great awakening. Rise up fearless preacher and declare the whole counsel of God.

No one in the Bible preached more on Hell than Jesus Himself, far more than heaven. So if it was good for the Master, it's good for His servants.

"Then will I teach transgressors Thy way; and sinners shall be converted unto Thee." (Psalm 51:13) God does not use dazzling angels to herald His truth, He uses redeemed sinners who have caught a glimpse of the yawning jaws of Hell ready to receive the lost.

There is a Heaven to gain but there is also a Hell to shun and if man will choose sin over the ever blessed Saviour; if sinners have made a covenant with death and with Hell, at least let us tell them of their doom and the wages of sin. Let us tell them about the worm that dieth not and fire that is not quenched. (Mark 9:46) Of weeping and of gnashing of teeth! (Luke 13:28) Damned souls ever dying, not living, existing yes, in Hell, ever dying, but never experiencing death. O, the torment: the drunk with his insatiable thirst for booze will cry out with very grief, but there will be no alcohol to abate his gnawing cravings. The sex fiend will howl like a mad dog, desiring but there will never be any satisfaction. The greedy will gnash their teeth as they grope for more but it will be like a mirage in the desert, it will vanish away like smoke but his greed will linger. The glutton will weep and howl like a maniac because of his lust for more but there is nothing to fill him. Every sin shall have its own proper torment. Then there are those of empty religion, mere pretenders, who sat through service after service and never came to the cross and believed. Through endless ages they will hear the echo of distant preachers pleading, "repent, repent", and they will remember how they spurned the call and trodden underfoot the Son of God and hath counted the blood of the covenant, wherewith he was sanctified, an unholy thing, and hath done despite unto the Spirit of grace. (Hebrews 10:29) False teachers and preachers will be there, "Lord, Lord, have we not prophesied in Thy name? And in Thy name cast out devils? And in Thy name done many wonderful works?" Then Jesus will profess unto them, "I never knew you: depart from me, ye that work iniquity for I never knew you." (Matthew 7:22,23) Think of the cruel mocking in Hell through endless ages by the damned, "Where is your incense now priest? Where is your creeds and your liturgy bishop? Where is your prosperity gospel of health and wealth now?" Also, rulers of nations and rulers of the people, who made men to tremble will tremble incessantly, like Belshazzar when he saw just the finger of God, so that the joints of his loins were loosed, and his knees smote one against another. (Daniel 5:6) Think of the madness as all the inmates of hell, which are made up of only the most wicked, miserable, horrible dregs and filth of all mankind. And to think, the sentence, if it were only for ten thousand years, there would be hope, but, it is for eternity. O that they might see it and turn. ETERNITY!

I preached a message like this one in a little Baptist church many years ago. The Spirit of God moved in that place in a very solemn way. When I gave the invitation there wasn't even a sound. But I looked out at the faces of the congregation and I saw husbands and wives grasp hands and with furrowed brows and tear streams they prayed like Hannah—their lips moved but no voice was heard. They were praying for their lost loved ones, "O, God have mercy upon them for thy grace and love's sake." If this doctrine does nothing else, may it at least burden our hearts to pray.

RESCUE THE PERISHING

Rescue the perishing; Care for the dying;
Snatch them in pity from sin and the grave.
Weep o'er the erring one; lift up the fallen;
Tell them of Jesus, the Mighty to save.

Rescue the perishing; Care for the dying.
Jesus is merciful; Jesus will save

Tho' they are slighting Him, Still He is waiting
Waiting the penitent child to receive.
Plead with them earnestly, Plead with them gently;
He will forgive if they only believe.

Down in the human heart, Crushed by the tempter,
Feelings lie buried that grace can restore.
Touched by a loving heart, wakened by kindness,
Chords that are broken will vibrate once more.

Rescue the perishing; Duty demands it.
Strength for thy labour the Lord will provide.
Back to the narrow way Patiently win them;
Tell the poor wand'rer a Saviour has died.

- Fanny Crosby (1832-1915)

CHAPTER 17

The Church

am convinced every single one of the church's spiritual ailments and woes can be cured by an earth shaking, heaven sent, sin hating, devil chasing, Holy Ghost revival.

- EDH

I came across this statement by Ravenhill and I chuckled because of his literary wit but the truth of it still brought it's piercing sting to my heart. "The church began with these men in the "upper room" agonizing—and today is ending in the supper room organizing. The church began in revival; we are ending in ritual. We started virile; we are ending sterile. Charter members of the church were men of heat and no degrees; today many hold degrees, but have no heat!"

It is death to a church that ceases to be an organism and becomes an organization. Stand before that little abandoned church house with boarded up windows and doors and ask, "What has happened?" I can hear the stones cry out and the beams creak as they seem to say, "This was once a good church. The word was faithfully preached, it's pews were filled with people singing songs of praise to Jesus. There were souls getting saved, lives were being changed, hearts were being purified by revival fires,... then, then the church became content to be a society, a social club, an organization. Oh, how the Holy Spirit was grieved and He vacated the premises. Great effort was made to attract people but no one was convinced there was any divine life

116

behind these walls and I have become a habitation of bats instead of a birthing place for souls."

Go, my friend, to the church of Sardis, stand before her rubble and inquire of her, "What is your pitiful story?" Oh, what a lamentable groan, as the rocks cry out, "We had a reputation that we were alive: we had activities, we had noise, we had enthusiasm, but we never addressed sin, we embraced worldliness, we catered to the flesh and all our births were only stillbirths; we ceased from being a living organism. We became a nice place to appease religious appetites, to improve our self worth, to feel alive, but now, Ichabod has become our name; the glory of the Lord departed. We are dead!"

A while ago the family was invited to sing at a Southern Ontario Church. We had a great night of ministry so I asked the pastor if we could return and preach a revival? He answered, "My church is so dead and cold, I don't think a revival would work." It was as if he were saying, "I have worked so hard to put these people into a deep sleep, I don't want anyone coming in here to disturb them."

To churches wanting revival,... I am using the words of the "father of modern day revival", Charles Finney. Modern, is a relative term, his ministry was in the early eighteen hundreds. He said, (and I'm paraphrasing) "God will not bring revival in any meaningful way, unless, the church takes a stance against the abominable practise of slavery." That of course was a major social issue of his day. But the second thing he said was, "That the church needed to take a stance against the use of alcohol", and Finney aught to know, because almost everywhere he preached there was revival. Today, I believe, unless we take a stance against the deplorable practise of abortion or the repulsive acts of homosexuality and sexual promiscuity there will be no revival. I am also in complete agreement with Finney, we must take a stance against alcohol and drugs or no revival. Finney said, "Do you not know that there are alcoholics hiding behind the fact that some pastors partake of alcohol or a deacon or respected member of the church?" Seriously, how important is revival to you.

Not long ago I sat through a sermon; it was a presentation of the gospel. I say it was a presentation because it was read, not preached. At the close of the message the brother reads his invitation, and in the same manner in which he would have read an announcement for signing up for the potluck. "If anyone thinks accepting Jesus as their Saviour is something they'd like to do, we will be up here at the front to talk to you." Dear reader, now I know there was only one George Whitefield but it was reported by one of his aids, that Mr Whitefield seldom ever completed a sermon without tears, at times it appeared he would not be able to finish the appeal. O, how he pleaded for lost sinners on their way to hell. "And now let me address all of you, high and low, rich and poor, one with another to accept mercy and grace while it is offered to you. Now is the accepted time, now is the day of salvation. And will you not accept it, now it is offered unto you? Do not stand out one moment longer. But come and accept of Jesus Christ...." Is it any wonder that God used this man to fetch souls for His kingdom.

I remember being invited to church by my neighbour. I remember being a very lost soul but thinking I was pretty good, pretty moral, and upright. I remember getting all gussied up in the suit I got married in, my wife and children (equally lost) were also beautifully dressed. I remember the warm people, the wonderful singing, and a sermon preached. Now, I am sure there were some who by our appearances thought we were good, solid Christians, but there were some who knew we were lost. The devil did not mind if my family and I went to church, he never had a problem with us being happy, or social, or moral or religious. He couldn't care less if we were pro life, or conservative, or even members of the church. The only thing he had a problem with, was the supernatural experience of the new birth. This church did all it could to make us happy, for us to meet new friends, to enjoy life, but I never heard the gospel preached; the devil would have been enraged. I was quite content in those days, but God had other plans. Our girls, ages five and eight, while in children's church were born again. Then was the foul fiend incensed.

A battle raged for our souls. It was then I dove into the scriptures, asked a myriad of questions, listened to Christian radio, until God visited me and I too was born again by the spirit of God, and my wife followed shortly after. The devil hated to lose one of his own, let alone an entire family.

Adam's likeness now efface,
Stamp Thine image In Thy place.

O the barrenness! I see spiritual tumbleweed,... have you noticed any in your church? It is what appears in a very dry and arid place. Dryness comes as a result of dry preachers, preaching dry messages, to dry boned congregations. Hooray, we know who the two witnesses are in the book of Revelation, and four riders of the apocalypse. Congratulations, we know our creed, our distinctives and countless other interesting truths, but if we are not knowing Jesus better, it is tumbleweed. We can be guilty of knowing the Word of God but not the God of the Word. Paul, said, "...that I might know Him..." (Philippians 3:10) Dear Lord, send the rain of REVIVAL.

Someone says, "Now we don't need to take this revival thing that serious, I mean,... we don't want to appear fanatical or weird or overly enthusiastic, I just don't think it's safe to take it too far. Right?" What will people think? Thus saith, the entire lukewarm church, whom Jesus warned He would spew [vomit] out of His mouth. (Revelation 3:16)

Question: what would it take to keep some of us from church this Lord's Day? If we're honest, what would it take? Someone says, "A headache, runny nose, or the possibility of a headache and a runny nose or just tired or a TV program, etc." Others have a stronger commitment, "Nothing!... Except tickets to the baseball game, football game, hockey game, or a fishing hole etc ..." Someone says, "Is this a problem? is this sin?" This simply reveals a problem. What would it take for you to miss church on a Monday or Tuesday night or a special meeting at 5:30 am before going off to work? If we're honest, we will admit it wouldn't take much. The problem is, many, for the most part, to some degree, have been just enduring church. Church is not meant to be endured but rather, to be embraced and enjoyed. When revival comes, there is nothing that will keep us away. A thirsting for God keeps us coming to the Fountain. This includes Bible reading, prayer, and evangelism, it is the natural outflow, no directions required.

A while ago a clean cut, nicely dressed, young man, carrying a bible approached me at my home. I immediately discerned this young man was not a Christian. How?... Because he was a clean cut, nicely dressed young man carrying a bible. The "Trendy" church has done away with these silly notions. Anyway, he asked me if I was interested in things of the bible? I replied, "Yes indeed! I love the truths of the Bible, (by this point I could tell he was a Jehovah's Witness) The Bible tells me of my Saviour's love and the ironclad hope I have of eternal life through His sacrifice on the cross". I then calmly proceeded to tell him, "The JWs are in the vilest of errors." He said, "In what way?" I then told him, "They err on: their interpretation of the one hundred and forty four thousand found in Revelation, the doctrine of the second coming of Christ, the deity of Jesus, the reward of heaven and the teachings on hell!" At which point he interrupted me and said, "Most people don't believe in hell anymore, regardless of their religion!" To which I replied, "This is very true, but I do! and the scriptures still declare it!" It's a sad day when these blind, polluters of truth can rebuke the church of Jesus Christ. Does anyone think we do not need revival? This young man is a JW not because he willfully loves lies but because the church never clearly presented the truth.

The great sin of the church is that, she has perpetuated infancy. We have for so long been fed a man centred message, that it has begun to taste normal. I agree, we must reach the spiritually young, but let us move on to maturity. We need solid, nurturing food for a ravished soul.

Hebrides Revival

The years following World War II had left the churches in the Hebrides Islands off the coast of Scotland with diminishing attendance. Not one church could boast of having a single young person. However, Peggy Smith, an eighty-four-year-old blind prayer warrior and her sister Christine turned their humble cottage, just on the outside of town, into a sanctuary of prayer for revival. Blind Peggy and her sister set their hearts to pray for revival and God began to prepare Duncan Campbell as His instrument. When Campbell had finished the first night of preaching, the awesome presence of God brought a wave of conviction of sin, that brought in groans of distress and prayers of repentance from the unconverted. Strong men were bowed down under the weight of sin and cries for mercy were mingled with shouts of joy from others who passed into life. There was a dance in progress that night and when the Spirit fell, the young people left the dance hall like they were fleeing from a plague and they made there way to the church. (Campbell, Peckham, Woolsey) Revival did come! Dear friends, this took place in 1949, just seventy one years ago; this is not ancient history; why can't we see another awakening?

We have the truth! Yes, there is an attack against it from all quarters, including the deluded churches, but we would expect that. If we were propagating a fairy tale, there would be no attack. We have the truth that sets men free and the enemy loves to see people in bondage. But I have no fear, why? Because I ask you,

Is a lie stronger than the truth?
Does a majority make a lie truth?
If I repeat a lie enough times will that make it true?
Can we vote a lie into the truth?
Do we believe the Word of God is truth?
When a lie is in direct opposition to God's revealed truth should we hold to the truth or compromise?

If we are labeled insensitive, bigoted, Neanderthal, phobic, intolerant, hateful,... etc, does that make a lie true? Friends, this old world embraces a lie, it tells us the Bible is outdated and irrelevant yet in spite of empirical evidence they tell us, there are more than two genders, we evolve from fish or lizards or germs,... it is crazy wrong. They hate God, His ways and His people: "The kings of the earth set themselves, and the rulers take counsel together, against the Lord and against His anointed saying. Let us break their bands asunder, and cast away their cords from us." (Psalm 2:2,3) "Woe unto them that call evil good, and good evil; that put darkness for light, and light for darkness; that put bitter for sweet, and sweet for bitter! Woe unto them that are wise in their own eyes, and prudent in their own sight!" (Isaiah 5:20,21) If they could, they would pull King Jesus from His rightful throne and crucify Him again. Yes, it looks bad but the truth shall prevail. May truth reign supreme in our hearts and also in the church, then let the sword of His mouth destroy the lies.

Church can never be about externals only, David understood that all his outward, religious, efforts could not fix the problem of his sinful backsliding. "For thou desirest not sacrifice; else would I give it." (Psalm 51:16) Make no mistake about it, unless sin is dealt with, God will not be impressed with our church attendance, our offering money, our posture of worship, or the formalities of our devotion. "The sacrifices of God are a broken spirit: a broken and contrite heart, O God thou wilt not despise." (Psalm 51:17) David is not saying our sobbing impresses God, but he is saying that true, heartfelt repentance will result in bitter contrition and then we can receive the blessedness of the sweet embrace of loving restoration.

Throughout church history, God has used the ministry of the evangelist to preach revival and evangelism. The evangelist is like a sheep dog, he works with the pastor (shepherd), he barks at the sheep; nips at their heels. His role is to chase the sheep through the sheep gate or back through the sheep gate. Now I know that in the 1970's and 80's the evangelists left a bad taste in the mouth of many churches. I met a retired pastor at a funeral, and my brother introduced me to him as an evangelist and when he heard that, he rolled his eyes back and mockingly said, "Oh my, you come in and scatter the flock and leave a mess for the pastor." I said, "not so, I will chase the wolf, I might scatter the goats but the sheep love and respect me." His problem was, the wolf and the goats had the money. But I fear, the modern day, trendy church has all but eradicated the ministry of the itinerant evangelist. Recently, I preached at a Christian camp in Canada and a woman told my wife that this was the first time she'd ever heard an evangelist. We will invite great gospel bands, or funny comedians, boring lifeless missionaries, or even mesmerizing magicians into the church house, but the devil will never tremble and quake for these. Now, if the church would let loose a fire breathing, Holy Ghost empowered evangelist on the platform, we might do some violence to the spirit of this world. Old farmer Charlie told me a long time ago, "The manure don't stink, until it's stirred up." We don't want things stirred up, we don't want things stinky, do we? Why?.... because we have embraced the spirit of this world as our lover. See 1 John 2:15-17.

Most of us, if not all of us, have had the distasteful experience of trying to carry on a conversation with someone while they are holding a cell phone, which is constantly dinging, indicating there is a text. It's a battle with distraction. I see in this a resemblance to the church, she seems easily distracted by the world and by the devil. Why do I say the only hope for a lost and dying world is a revived church?... because if the bride is not concentrated and enamoured with the Bridegroom how can we expect the world to be interested. They will only ridicule us as having a pretend love. Jesus is looking for the genuine article and so is the perishing world.

The church revived will evangelize. Don't get me wrong, whatever you can learn about soul winning, learn. But what I am saying is, in times of revival, the church will do away with evangelism classes. The revelation of the risen and glorified Saviour will compel us to say like the apostles, "For we cannot but speak the thing which I have seen and heard." (Acts 4:20) Or, like the prophet Isaiah when he saw the Lord high and lifted up, we will declare, "Here am I; send me". (Isaiah 6:8) The church revived will evangelize.

David Brainerd, and Robert Murray M'Cheyne had a few

things in common: one of them was, they never saw their thirtieth birthdays. They were bright, burning torches for Jesus. God does not keep men like these around for a long time; they illuminate exceedingly bright for a time and are extinguished. Most of us are like little candles; we may burn for sixty or seventy years but we only throw a little light. O that revival fire would set us a blaze for Jesus. O that the church might again be like the city on a hill. O that it would give light to all that are lost in the world.

Patrick Henry's speech at the Virginia Convention, March 23, 1775: "Is life so dear or peace so sweet as to be purchased at the price of chains and slavery? Forbid it, Almighty God! I know not what course others may take. But as for me, give me liberty —or give me death!"

Listen to Ravenhill's Christianized rendition and weep: "Is life's span so dear and are home comforts so engrossing as to be purchased with my unfaithfulness and dry-eyed prayerlessness? At the final bar of God, shall the perishing millions accuse me of materialism coated with a few Scripture verses? Forbid it, Almighty God! I know not what course others may take; but as for me, GIVE ME REVIVAL in my soul and in my church and in my nation—or GIVE ME DEATH!"

The Welsh Revival of 1904

The pastor, at the end of the regularly scheduled Monday night prayer meeting, asked those who were interested, to stay behind for a few moments, while a young man by the name of Evan Roberts addressed them. He gave four sentences to the seventeen people that remained behind.

1. You must put away all unconfessed sin.
2. You must put away any doubtful habits.
3. You must obey the Holy Spirit promptly.
4. You must confess Christ publicly.

All seventeen agreed and this sparked the Welsh revival of 1904-1905 that ushered in an estimated one hundred and fifty thousand souls into God's family. My beloved church, can we not see, do we not hear, Mr. Robert's message is for us today, it is for the here and Now! For who hath despised the day of small things? (Zechariah 4:10)

Pentecost

The greatest revival ever experienced was when the church was birthed, on the day of Pentecost. In some ways, this revival still reverberates to the present time. Martin Lloyd-Jones said, "It is a truism to say that every revival of religion that the church has ever known has been, in a sense, a kind of repetition of what happened on the day of Pentecost." Ah, but what did it look like? Pentecost began in weakness, and ended in power. It began with a hundred and twenty and ended with over three thousand souls. It began with a ten day prayer meeting, of pouring out one's soul, and ended with the outpouring of the Holy Ghost. It began with the Holy Hum of prayer but it ended with the sound of a rushing mighty wind. It began with the cold bewilderment of anticipation and ended with tongues of fire. It began with unlearned and ignorant men and ended with men who were endued with knowledge and could speak in any language of the people present. It began with mocking, and confusion and ended with the words, "What shall we do? It began with empty religiosity and ended with a deep, heart felt repentance. Men and women were added to the church and they continued steadfastly in the apostles doctrine. Herein lies our pattern.

A shipwrecked mariner on a desolate island rejoices to see footprints in the sand. Somebody has already trod the sandy beaches. We have a long history and a concise record of revivals. Look down the long corridor of the history of revival and you will see. The biblical record: the judges, the prophets, the kings, Pentecost, and the apostles. Church history: in every century, God poured out His Spirit in revival, revivals led by men like Savonarola, Hus, Luther, Whitefield, Wesley, Finney, Moody, Spurgeon, Sunday, Campbell and many others. We are just placing our feet into the prints of those who have gone before us.

Dr Orr, the revivalist preacher and writer of the song "Cleanse Me" was lecturing at Columbia International University in South Carolina, when a young man requested an appointment. Orr agreed to see him in the lobby of the men's dormitory. The young man reported that Orr, perhaps shy, seemed uncomfortable with the interview. Instead of looking in his direction and engaging in conversation, he gazed straight ahead and answered the questions with short replies. After fruitless exchanges, the young man decided to ask him one last thing.

"Dr. Orr, besides praying for revival, what can I do to help bring it about?" Without a moment's pause, he glanced in the young man's direction and gave an answer he did not expect nor would he ever forget: "You can let it begin with you."

-excerpt from "Then Sings My Soul" Robert J. Morgan

"Go home", says Rodney "Gypsy" Smith, "Lock yourself in your room. Kneel down in the middle of the floor; and with a piece of chalk draw a circle around yourself. There, on your knees, pray fervently and brokenly that God would start revival within that chalk circle."

Cleanse Me

O Holy Ghost revival comes from thee;
Send a revival,
Start the work in me.

- J. Edwin Orr

CHAPTER 18

Evangelism

> *evival begins by Christians getting right first and then spills over into the world.*
>
> *- CH Spurgeon*

As I have already stated previously, revival is alway connected to evangelism. Revival is the experience that revolutionizes the church: evangelism is the expression of the church that reaches the world.

The apostle Paul wrote, "I am made all things to all men, that I might by all means save some. (1Corinthians 9:22b)" Back in the early days of our ministry we had this text displayed on our trailer. It was never the apostle Paul's aim to simply moralize, or to instruct sinners how to improve, but that they might be saved. Moralized, churched sinners enter the same hell as murderers, thieves and harlots. To reform the lost is as futile as painting a sinking ship.

"Why, Mr. Whitefield," inquired a friend one day, "why do you so often preach on, 'Ye must be born again.'"? "Because" replied Mr. Whitefield, looking solemnly into the face of his questioner, "Ye must be born again"!

There was a time when Mr. Evangelist came to preach at the Church of the Sleepyhead. It was a thunderous message replete with seraphic images of heaven and dolorous cries from the pit of hell. When the invitation was given, several were awakened, ten souls placed their faith on the merits of Jesus alone, and several felt revival in their hearts. There were however, twelve members of the church that indicated they would no longer be staying at Sleepyhead. Mr. Drowsy, was quoted as saying, "How dare this man come to our church and disturb the peace!" Mrs. In-My-Opinion, chimed in, "I hate Mr. Evangelist!... He's loud, abrasive, brash, and far too impassioned!" Ms. I-Like-It-Watered-down, added her two cents, retorting, "I think toning things down would suit me far better." Mr. Formalist, mentioned, "The whole night was very— undignified!" While Mrs. Feelings, protested by the comment, "He made me feel uncomfortable!" They all agreed, "We will take our membership to the First Comfy Church." I wonder, after the dust settles, where the focus will rest, on the souls saved, or the baggage lost.

Revival is our only hope for a barren church and a dying world. Historically, revival has always been God's remedy and besides, we have tried every other way and means and they have all failed. The trendy church may be growing outward but is there any depth? Travail is hard, labour is hard but it is all we got. If we are to see revival, we must put our spiritual backs into it, or better said, our whole hearts: without reserve.

Two Salvation Army officers set out on a campaign in Los Angeles California, in the 1920s, their new work seemed to be met with only failure and opposition. Frustrated and tired they appealed to the General, William Booth, to close the rescue mission. Booth sent back a telegram with two words on it, "TRY TEARS." They followed the advice and they witnessed a mighty revival.

After the death of Robert Murray M'Cheyne a man came to visit the famed church where M'Cheyne preached. The sexton showed him around, "Sit down here," said the sexton, leading him to the chair where M'Cheyne used to sit. "Now put your elbows on the table." The visitor obeyed. "Now put your face in your hands," The visitor obeyed again. "Now let the tears flow,....that was the way Mr. M'Cheyne used to do." Then the amazed visitor was led to the very pulpit where the impassioned M'Cheyne once poured out his soul to God and poured out God's message to the people. "Put your elbows on the pulpit. " instructed the old sexton. The elbows were put in place. "Put your face in your hands." The young man obeyed. "Now let the tears flow."....that was the way Mr. M'Cheyne used to do." To do much for God, we must be much with God. (Story told by C.H. Spurgeon) This is what authentic soul stirring evangelism looks like.

I want you to listen to this plea for sinners, to believe on the Lord Jesus Christ from some of our modern preachers. "If you should die in your sins, it will be eternal separation from God." Is that not sort of like saying to an anarchist, "If you continue in this path of destruction, you will most certainly have a society without government." Or to a thief, "Turn from your evil ways, or you will be faced with an existence without police." To the enemy of God, being separated from God is his delight. We can remove Hell from our minds, but we never can remove it from holy scripture. O for men of the Word who will fetch souls for the kingdom.

In every evangelistic meeting I have ever been involved in, I held to the biblical order of: believe, behave, belong. I have however, over the years, noticed a shift of the order to: belong, that is, to make a sinner feel comfortable and accepted. Behave, that is, to encourage a sinner to try to live like a Christian: through endless sermons on how to fix your marriage, or how to improve your bank account, or how to live happy lives and then, they are admonished to believe, or somehow, belief is just supposed to happen by osmosis. Someone says, "What's the problem?" What do we call someone who is part of the church, and participating in all the disciplines of the church but has not the Spirit of God dwelling in them? The Bible calls them Pharisees. Jesus said, "...for ye make clean the outside of the cup and the platter but your inward part is full of ravening and wickedness." (Luke 11:39). "...thou blind Pharisees, cleanse first that which is within the cup and the platter, that the outside of them may be clean also." (Matthew 23:26) We could be unintentionally making modern day Pharisees. It must be heard plainly, "Flee the wrath to come, flee the wrath to come, flee the wrath to come,"(Luke

3:7) How? Believe on the Lord Jesus Christ, never let salvation be anything more than that, Believe!

Martha said, "Lord by this time he stinketh: for he hath been dead four days." (John 11:39) Lazarus needs revival. Now we could take Lazarus out of the tomb, we could dress him up real pretty like, we could set him in the pew, we could prop him up with all kinds of activities, and social programs, we could sing to him until we are blue in the face, we could have the latest and greatest platform with all the trendy media equipment. (Comfort) We could even change the name of the church, Um,... how about, "Rock Alive", and make it sound less "churchy" but dear friend, until Lazarus hears the voice of the Son of God there is no life in him. O, for a revelation of Christ in His church!

I read a collection of sermons by Robert Murray M'Cheyne, the man who preached with eternity stamped on his brow. He preached to a congregation of eleven hundred people, between the years 1836 and 1843 in St Peter's Church, Dundee Scotland, at which time he left this world and went to be with his master. The one thing that stands out to me, is he seemed to preach as if he believed that no one in his congregation was saved. Even while he was in a state of delirium, on the brink of eternity, he seemed to plead and pray for the souls of his flock. Someone says, "But surely he must have been wrong." Ah, but how much better it is to err like M'Cheyne, than like the pillow prophets of today, who believe everyone to be saved by virtue of the fact they are in church.

Benjamin Franklin, a cold blooded, calculating philosopher, said of the evangelist George Whitefield, "It was wonderful to see the change made by his preaching in the manner of the inhabitants of Philadelphia. From being thoughtless or indifferent about religion, it seemed as if the whole world were growing religious." Ravenhill writes, "What was the secret of his preaching?... he preached a pure gospel, he preached a powerful gospel, he preached a passionate gospel."

We had an opportunity to sing and preach at a men's prison. We set up our equipment and then the Chaplin asked to speak to me. He questioned me with a stern voice and a furrowed brow, "How do you preach?" (I think he heard a rumour about my preaching.) I replied, "I'm sorry, What do you mean?" He, clearly agitated, stated, "We will have none of that hellfire and brimstone preaching around here." (I think he was looking to keep his "shut out", that is, souls shut out of heaven.) "These men" said he, "Don't need condemnation, they need love and acceptance, these poor men are victims of society." I then calmly answered, "I preach grace, I preach the good news of the gospel of Jesus Christ. However, (now slightly more impassioned) I also preach the bad news: that man is not a victim but a rebel, he is an anarchist in his heart, that he is worthy of hell and damnation." I abruptly continued, "If that doesn't fit your approval we will be on our way." He reluctantly said it was too late now, please go ahead. After the sermon, God awakened eight souls and they all registered for discipleship classes through another ministry. Thankfully not through that fox.

But I hear someone say, "I've read your thoughts on revival and I don't like them. You're divisive, unkind and too severe!" My response is, if you are an unbeliever, a pretender, a self righteous Pharisee, or a blatant rebel, I tell you the truth, I am not one fraction as severe as King Jesus. It is turn or burn! But I hear someone else claim, "I am a Christian; churched all my life; my God would never send anybody to Hell." My answer, You are absolutely correct, because your god does not exist. You are an idolater, you have created a snuggly cuddly god, a god of your own imagination, and my advice is still the same. TURN OR BURN! "But", says another, "Do we really need all this talk about revival," Listen, yes, emphatically, yes, until we have revival. May it be constantly on our lips, and continually in our prayers. "O that thou wouldst revive us again."

Personal Evangelism

We are all called, in some way, to evangelism, "He that wins souls is wise." We must all be ready to tell the good news of the gospel. For it is the power of God unto salvation.

I am not going to guilt anyone into evangelism, it doesn't work, but, the soul revived, will evangelize, he cannot help but speak the thing which he has seen and heard. The reality is, we have never personally ever seen anyone physically cast into a burning Hell, we have never caught a glimpse of the languishing, tormented souls in the bottomless pit, and our minds are loathed to even briefly glance at the Great White Throne Judgment,—the problem is, we do not even hear about it anymore. "His watchmen are blind, they are all dumb dogs, they cannot bark." (Isaiah 56:10). Where are those who will sound the trumpet, "The Alarm of War!"(Jeremiah 4:19) Where are the sons of thunder! Where then is our motivation to rescue the perishing and to care for the dying. Knowing the terror of the Lord we persuade men. (2 Corinthians 5:11)

D.L. Moody approached a man in the streets of Chicago and enquired of him, "Are you a Christian?" The man replied, "It is none of your business!" To which Moody insisted, "It is my business!" "Oh" said the man, "Then you must be D.L. Moody"

So, what is personal evangelism? It is the act of sharing the gospel one on one, which I have found to be one of the evidences of true revival. When revival invigorates the soul, you cannot help but share the good news to others. Out of us will flow rivers of living water.(John 7:38)

Personal evangelism also sparks revival. Try talking to someone about what Jesus has done for you. Now, make no mistake about it, there will be much spiritual opposition but when you actually open your mouth and simply tell someone about your faith in Jesus it will begin to fan a revival flame in your own heart. Try it!

One does not need to be a theologian to witness for Jesus, (though we all should be theologians, i.e. the science of God), we need only do as any other witness does in a courtroom on a witness stand. You simply, in your own words, recount what happened. To witness for Jesus is simply to recount what Jesus has done for you. I once was lost but now I'm found; I was blind but now I see.

Personal evangelism is:
More listening than speaking.
More living out our faith than describing it.
More love displayed than lectures given.
More language of prayer than the tongue of pride.
More literature of Holy writ than the wisdom of this world.

"If any man thirst." (John 7:37). Thirst is the word used when there is a lack of fluid in the body. A thirsty person does not need to know the chemical and molecular properties of water, or the physiological function of the body to receive it, he only needs to know, he needs water. A man could die of thirst while on a lifeboat, floating on Lake Ontario: he could die of thirst standing in water up to his neck. As long as he does not take in water, he will die. He must drink, he must come to the fountain, Jesus said, "...come unto me and drink..." (John 7:37) and He will satisfy the thirsty soul. The problem the Pharisees had, was they had to come to the same fountain and drink of the same water as the prostitutes, the thieves, the drunks, and the publicans. There is no other way. Let us show our fellow man, let us tell them where to find water for a thirsty soul. The place where we ourselves found mercy and grace, in the crimson river of life; in the wounds of Jesus. No one can argue with what Jesus did for you.

Pray for opportunities, pray for the power of God in your witness, seek help if you need it, find a way to be an effective witness but the best way is to be always at the fountain, living in a state of revival perpetually.

A while ago, the family was invited to preach and sing at a revival. The church provided for our meals by having a different family each day host lunches and suppers at their homes. We were treated like royalty. At the revival meetings, as was our practice, (and still is) we presented our musical package, and the sermon, in a demonstrative and passionate way. About three days into the revival, the pastor approached me, "Brother", said he, as he stared at the ground and as he softly kicked the dirt, "we have had a few complaints,... some people have thought you were a little, well, 'showy'". "Hmmm", I pondered for a second, as I scratched my bearded chin, "I see" — Then I continued, "By the way, may I tell you how wonderful your church has treated us. We have dined sumptuously, with the best gold rimmed plates, the best of pewter ware, the finest cutlery, the most delicate crystal and the most delicious meals." He, in delightful surprise and bursting with pride, replied, "Really, my church has done all that?" "Yes,... But" I interrupted, "Don't you find it all a little... 'showy'." He thought a little bit, and a smile came across his face and he conceded, "Point well taken." And whatever ye do, do it heartily, as to the Lord...(Colossians 3:23) The Lord is looking for those who will pull out the stops. You might be saying, "I'm not good at witnessing," You do not have to be good, just available, "but I'm shy," Well then, do me a favour, intercede in prayer for me. Maybe you are not like the brave fireman who unflinchingly runs into a burning building to save precious lives, but you can pray for him,... pray for me, pray for your pastor, pray for the soul winners in your church, with importunity: heartily. There is likely more good done in the prayer closet, than in proclaiming the word in the work of evangelism. I am reminded that God can raise up what or who He wants to be heralds of His message. He used a donkey to rebuke the headstrong prophet, (numbers 22:28) an ant to preach to the slothful, (Proverbs 6:6-8) even the heavens declare the glory of the Lord and the firmament showeth His handiwork, (Psalm 19:1-4) but I have never heard of God using anything or anyone but frail humanity to offer up prayers and supplications at the throne of grace. Dear prayer warrior your name may never be recognized in the church but it will be in Hell. The demons said, "Jesus I know and Paul I know...." (Acts 19:13) My plea is that you be part of the evangelism machine, whole heartedly and without reserve. My hope is when you pray or open your mouth and share the gospel, all the demons in hell will shudder.

Ah Lord God,
You who are maker and sustainer of all things.
You who made the world, and all that is in it, work in my heart.
You who created the heavens and the earth from nothing,
My heart is nothing, create in me something that will glorify and honour you.
Make my life, which is like a desert, rejoice and blossom like as a rose for you.
Take my mind,
My thoughts,
My works,
My desires,
My dreams,
My hopes,
My aspirations,
Recreate them, so that they are wholly yours.
Keep me from my backsliding by the word of your sustaining power.
May I see that in you is life, joy, love, and peace and that without you, I am without form, and void, and darkness is upon the face of the depth of my soul.
- EDH

CHAPTER 19

Final Thoughts

> *here is no sin so great that God's presence can't revive his church... We can have the greatest revival in the history of Christianity if we will only seek it.*
>
> *-Douglas Porter*

O, dear friend, how I love revival meetings but it's not enough. We need revival! O, how I long for the Holy Ghost to come and in a very real way awaken us again. But there needs to be an attitude adjustment before we have an altitude adjustment. As long as we think things are acceptable, we will never seek revival. The longer we go without revival the less we will seek it, pray for, or even consider it for our day.

I hear someone mockingly chide, "Hey brother, What do you think this book will do for the church?" My answer, I honestly do not know, but I pray this little book shows us where we are and where we ought to be. But let me just add this, everything I wrote about revival is absolutely true whether you liked it, believed it, or not.

Dear reader, are you a Christian? I mean, are you trusting in the merits of Jesus alone? If I have written this book and you still are not saved, my heart will break in two. I desperately desire you to come to Jesus in simple childlike faith and say, "Nothing in my hands I bring but simply to the cross I cling." What stops you? He has promised, if you will come, with just your sin to the cross, The blood of Jesus

Christ God's Son cleanseth us from all sin. (1John 1:7) Will you not turn from your sin and turn to Jesus...please!

The old man stood outside the general store in the middle of the little mountainous village. This was the ideal spot to chat with the townsfolk and perhaps receive a few pennies, nickels or dimes for his beggar's cup. That day the fog descended quickly on the quaint little town and time had taken wings and flew away. So, the old man began his trek home. His eyes had grown dim with age, his gate slow as he shuffled along and the fog and darkness made travelling much more difficult than normal. Although he had made this journey many times before, he suddenly became disoriented. There were no sounds or smells to guide him this day and the signs along the road were futile to him. Then, he had a strange feeling that he knew the way. He began to boldly walk, absolutely certain he was going in the right direction. The direction however, was wrong, he was heading right toward a cliff, which had a sharp descent. There were warning signs but he could not see them. Forty feet to the edge, thirty feet to the edge, twenty feet to the edge. He stopped but for a moment, questioning his decision but he thought within himself, "no, I'm sure this is right, it just feels right."... Now he is five feet from the precipice, one step after another until the last step leads him headlong, down, down, down the great chasm where he is dashed to pieces and perishes.

You are that old beggar. Life has caught up with you. You thought you had lots of time but suddenly a fog descends. The devil has blinded you. There are warnings but you have either ignored them or you are insensible to them. Now is the time to turn to Jesus. Look to the crucified Christ, Look unto him and be ye saved. You say, "I feel I'm going the right way, I will trust my instincts". Have your instincts ever failed you? They are wrong now, don't trust your feelings, trust the Truth. Jesus died for sinners, blind sinners like you. Believe in Him alone and thou shalt be saved. Do not, I repeat, do not let another day go by without being saved. You may be forty feet or you may be one step from the brink of eternity. You reach into your pockets to fish for a few tokens and pull out your hands with nothing in them but a bit of fluff. There is nothing you can give, a billionaire could not afford it, but you can have it. Come, come, buy without money and without price. Jesus paid it all. ETERNITY! Dear Christian I have a word for you too. There is revival for you, there is revival for the church. I know not when it will come. I do know we need it. Will you not seek God, will you not pray, and believe Him? Shall not the Lamb that was slain receive the reward for His suffering. Shall not the almighty God receive glory, honour and praise?

One last word, and I direct this to you dear saints who has battled hard over the years seeking revival at the glorious hand of God. You can show me the dings in your armour, when the enemy had buffeted you with lance and spear but your breastplate of righteousness has held strong. You can point out the dents in your helmet, Oh, how you were knocked silly, your vision blurred, you were dizzy for awhile but the helmet of salvation was never knocked off. Your shield of faith shows the black, sooty marks from the flaming darts and your sword is chipped in a few places but there you stand. I salute you brave warrior of the cross, fight on. May our coat of arms read, "Non nobis domine no nobis sed nomini tuo do gloriam." "Not to us Lord, not to us but to Thy name let the glory be given." (Psalm 113:1) Semper Fi

If God has visited you through the inward working of His Spirit, and has brought to you salvation through the merits of Jesus Christ alone, or has ignited revival in your heart, please let us know that we may have the privilege of rejoicing with you. For further information about Hilton Ministries, please contact us at: hiltonministries94@gmail.com